What's Chemistry all about?

Alex Frith & Dr. Lisa Jane Gillespie
Illustrated by Adam Larkum

Designed by Steve Wood, Anna Gould,
Samantha Barrett & Tom Lalonde

Chemistry consultant: Dr. John Spokes
Edited by Rosie Dickins & Jane Chisholm
Series advisor: Tony Payton

Contents

Internet links

You can find out lots more about chemistry on the internet. You can find out about every single element, do experiments in an online lab, and build your very own molecules. For links to these websites, and many more, go to www.usborne-quicklinks.com and type in the keywords "what is chemistry".

The links are regularly reviewed and updated, but Usborne Publishing cannot be responsible for any website other than its own. Please follow the internet safety guidelines displayed on the Usborne Quicklinks Website.

What's chemistry all about?

Chemistry is all about different types of stuff – or **substances**, to use a scientific word. It's about what substances are, what they can do, what's inside them and how they can change. Chemists study all kinds of substances – from everyday things, like mud and smoke, to rare, deadly ones like strong acids and explosive powders.

Chemists are constantly asking questions and doing experiments to find the answers. The answers may reveal what something is made of, or show what it can do. Here are some of the questions chemists ask...

Lab rules

Chemists don't always wear white coats. But if they're working with messy substances, they wear clothes that they don't mind getting dirty. And if they're using dangerous substances, they wear gloves and goggles for protection.

What exactly IS this stuff?

How do you really know what anything is? A bottle of liquid labelled 'water' might not really contain water. To find out what a mystery substance is, a chemist asks more questions.

> What on earth IS this?

> How heavy is it?

What does it DO?

Different substances do different things. For example, pure water boils at 100°C. Chemists call this one of the **properties** of water. Other properties include toughness, and how easily it mixes with other substances.

> Do things dissolve in it?

> What happens if you heat it up?

Is it just one thing?

Some substances are made of just one thing, but others are a mixture of various different things. A chemist might need to break something down into its different parts before working out what each part is made of.

What is this gooey stuff?

I think it's a mixture.

Can I change it into something else?

Many substances can be used to create other substances. Sometimes they will change if you heat them up, but mostly they change when they are mixed with other substances. This change is called a **reaction**.

What happens if I mix this with this?

What can I change this into?

What makes it change?

Can I change it back again?

Finding all the answers

Chemists know a lot about substances, but they don't know everything. Ever since people began doing experiments, they've discovered more and more new substances, and more ways to use them.

Turn the page to find some of the interesting and useful inventions that chemists have been responsible for.

Things chemists don't know... yet.

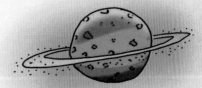

What about all those substances on alien planets? Are they like the ones on Earth, or are they completely different?

How have chemists changed the world?

Chemists are always experimenting with substances, mixing them together, heating them up, and testing them to see what they can do. And sometimes this results in remarkable inventions. Here are just a few of the amazingly useful things that chemists have given to the world.

Batteries

A battery provides electricity. Inside, pieces of two different metals are placed apart in a liquid or paste. The metals react with the liquid, making an electric charge flow.

Some of the earliest experiments with batteries were performed by Italian Alessandro Volta in 1791.

Volta's first experiment gave him a shock.

Silver spoon

Tin rod

Salt water

Matches

Matches are tipped with a mixture of substances that will catch fire when struck against a rough surface.

Early matches caught fire too easily. The first 'safety matches' were invented in 1827 by Englishman John Walker.

Petrol engine

Engines are machines that make things move – such as cars. But they need power to operate. In 1870, Austrian scientist Siegfried Marcus hit upon the idea of using petrol as a fuel to make an engine run – an early version of a motor vehicle.

The colourful story of mauve

One day in 1856, chemist William Perkin was cleaning up after a messy experiment, when something strange happened...

Perkin called his new colour 'mauve'. At the time, there was no cheap way to manufacture purple dye.

I'll wash this gunk out with alcohol.

Ooooh! It's gone a lovely purple colour.

I can make some serious money out of this...

Mauve became fashionable after Queen Victoria wore it.

White paint

Paint contains coloured substances called pigments. The pigment titanium dioxide is bright white, and is used in house paints.

Titanium dioxide occurs naturally, and has been used to manufacture paint since the 1920s.

Antifreeze

A chemical called ethylene glycol is the main ingredient in liquid antifreeze. It forms a layer of liquid on a car windscreen and won't freeze even when it's very cold.

Non stick pans

In 1938, American Roy Plunkett was trying to make a refrigerator chemical, but instead his experiments produced a useful new plastic. His team called it Teflon®.

When they get hot, most things become sticky – but Teflon® doesn't. It is used to coat cooking pans.

Inhalers

Since the 1960s, many people with asthma have used inhalers to help them during an attack. Inhalers contain the substance salbutamol, which relaxes the breathing muscles and stops the attack.

Heat packs

A liquid called sodium acetate is very useful to mountain climbers. They carry small packs filled with it on their hikes. When they want to warm up, they press a button on the pack which releases solid sodium acetate into the liquid. This makes the liquid turn into crystals, and gives out heat.

Digital cameras

When you take a photo, light entering a digital camera causes a chemical reaction in a light-sensitive substance. This reaction produces an electric charge.

The camera changes this charge into a code and uses a series of codes to store or display the photo.

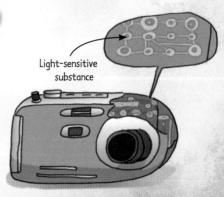

Light-sensitive substance

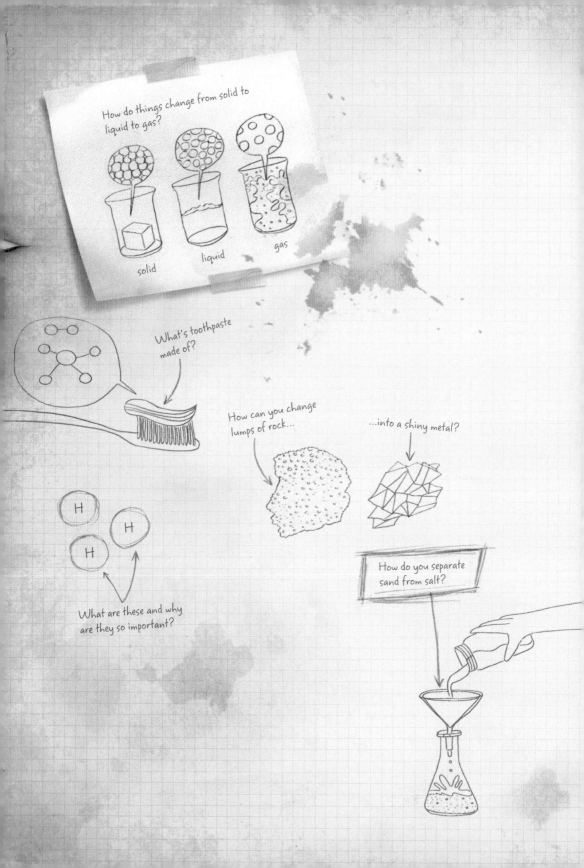

Part 1:

What's the world made of?

The Universe is full of a wide range of different substances – from hard, shiny metals and beautiful, crystal diamonds, to soft, bendy plastics and black, crumbly coal. But, deep, deep down, everything is made of the same thing – mindbogglingly tiny specks called **atoms**. Read on to find out more...

Meet your first atom...

Chemists often draw atoms as simple circles. This circle with an 'H' in it represents a single atom of an element called hydrogen.

Simple symbols

Chemists use symbols for each different kind of atom so they can write them down quickly. You can see a list of them all on pages 30-31.

Meet your second atom...

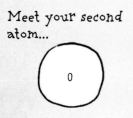

An *atom* of oxygen

...and your first molecule.

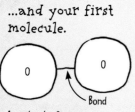

A *molecule* of oxygen

What's an atom?

You can think of atoms as incredibly small building blocks. There are 117 kinds of atom. Substances can be very simple or quite complicated, depending on how many kinds of atom they're made of. The simplest substances, called **elements,** are made of only one kind of atom.

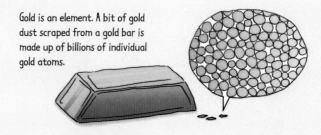

Gold is an element. A bit of gold dust scraped from a gold bar is made up of billions of individual gold atoms.

Even huge blocks of gold only contain individual gold atoms. But atoms in most other substances stick together in groups of two or more atoms called **molecules**.

What are molecules?

Molecules are made when atoms make links called **bonds** between each other. For example, oxygen atoms bond in pairs to make molecules of oxygen – which is found naturally in the air.

Atoms don't have to bond with the same kind of atom. A molecule of water is made of two atoms of hydrogen bonded with one atom of oxygen. Although water – like every other substance – is made of atoms, there's no such thing as an atom of water. That's because the smallest amount of water you can have, that is still water, is a *molecule*. Because water contains more than one kind of atom, it's not an element – it's something called a **compound**.

10

Forming compounds

Compounds can only be created when substances mix together and undergo a **chemical reaction** (you can find out more about this on page 34).

A reaction can make elements bond together and form an entirely new chemical substance, which behaves differently from the elements that made it.

Do reactions always happen when you mix substances?

No. Elements and compounds can also mix without reacting or bonding together. This creates another kind of substance known as a **mixture**. Most things in our world are mixtures. For example, air is a mixture of gases, and mud is a mixture of soil, stones, leaves and all sorts.

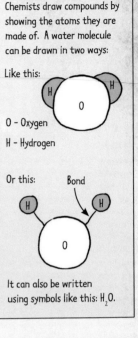

Compound sketch

Chemists draw compounds by showing the atoms they are made of. A water molecule can be drawn in two ways:

Like this:

H O H

O - Oxygen

H - Hydrogen

Or this: Bond

H   H

O

It can also be written using symbols like this: H_2O.

Elements are made of only one kind of atom. This is a molecule of nitrogen, with two nitrogen atoms in it.

Compounds are made of more than one kind of atom bonded together.

They can be quite complicated, like this molecule of sulphuric acid.

In a mixture, such as mud, different elements and compounds are jumbled up, but they haven't bonded with each other.

Bits of plants and animals

Stones and rocks

Air

Water

Mud is a mixture of many different substances.

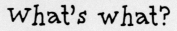

What's what?

All the substances in the Universe are elements, mixtures or compounds. Here are a few examples...

Oxygen molecule

Oxygen

Oxygen is an **element**. It's one of the gases in the air we breathe. It reacts easily with other elements, which means it's also found in many compounds.

Carbon dioxide

Carbon dioxide is a **compound** of carbon and oxygen. It's a gas in the air which plants use to make food.

Carbon dioxide molecule

Iron oxide molecule

Iron ore

Iron ore is a **mixture**. It's mostly a compound called iron oxide, mixed with some other bits. It can be dug out of the ground, and then processed to extract pure iron.

Water molecule

Water

Pure water is a **compound** of oxygen and hydrogen – and nothing else.

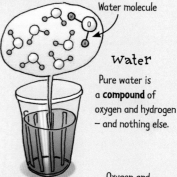

Milk

Milk is a **mixture** of lots of compounds. It's mainly water, with a mix of fat, sugar and minerals such as calcium, which we need for healthy teeth and bones.

Other minerals — Calcium
Fat
Sugar
Water

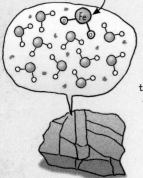

Sea water

Sea water is a **mixture**. It's mainly water, but it also has salt and oxygen and other bits dissolved in it. Fish breathe the dissolved oxygen through their gills.

Oxygen and lots of minerals
Salt
Water

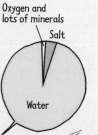

Human beings

Your blood is mainly a **mixture** of two compounds – an iron-based compound, called hemoglobin, and water. It also contains small amounts of oxygen, carbon dioxide, nitrogen, sodium and chlorine.

Other

Hemoglobin

Water

Sweetener

Calcium carbonate molecule

Toothpaste

Toothpaste is a **mixture** of two compounds called sodium fluoride (which strengthens your teeth) and calcium carbonate (which rubs away stains). It also contains detergents, sweeteners and dyes, to keep your teeth clean and shiny and your breath fresh.

Sodium fluoride molecule

Vinegar

Vinegar is often used to flavour food. Its chemical name is ethanoic acid. It's a **compound** of carbon, hydrogen and oxygen.

Ethanoic acid molecule

Milk of magnesia

Milk of magnesia is a **mixture** of two compounds: magnesium hydroxide and water. Magnesium hydroxide cancels out stomach acids that can cause indigestion. The water is just to make it drinkable.

Magnesium hydroxide molecule

Water molecule

Acetone

Acetone is a **compound** of carbon, hydrogen and oxygen. It's a liquid that can be used to remove nail varnish or to weaken glue.

Acetone molecule

Glues

Most glues are **mixtures** of some sticky, runny compounds (such as cyanoacrylate, which contains carbon, hydrogen, oxygen and nitrogen) and smelly liquids (such as ethyl acetate which contains carbon, hydrogen and oxygen) that slowly dry and harden.

Ethyl acetate molecule

Cyanoacrylate molecule

Getting in a state

Substances can exist in one of three different **states**; as a **solid**, **liquid** or **gas**. Most substances can be found in all of these states — but not at the same time. Take water, for example. It's usually a liquid, but it can also be a solid (ice) or a gas (steam) — it all depends on the temperature.

Why does temperature matter?

One of the strangest things that chemists have discovered is that nothing is ever completely still. Take a solid block of wood. You may not be able to see it moving, but in fact the atoms and molecules it's made of are constantly fidgeting and moving around. How much they move depends on how much heat there is.

When molecules are cold, they don't have much energy, so they sit tightly packed and form a solid. But even then they vibrate slightly, in their fixed positions.

Molecules that are a bit warmer have more energy and move away from each other, forming a liquid. They can move enough so the liquid can flow.

Really hot, energetic molecules can fly far apart from each other. This is what's going on in a gas.

Meet mercury

Mercury is the only metal that is liquid at room temperature. It won't freeze until -39°C, and it doesn't boil until it reaches an incredibly high 357°C.

Mercury is often used to measure temperature. As mercury gets hotter, it expands. When it's inside a thermometer with markings on the side, you can see exactly how much the mercury expands, and that tells you what the temperature is.

Absolute cold

Chemists think that if you could make the temperature really low — as low as -273.15°C — atoms would stop moving completely. They call this absolute zero. They can make things very nearly, but not quite, this cold — so we don't know for sure.

Ice (solid)

Water (liquid)

Steam (gas)

Changing state

Most susbtances have their own temperature at which they change from one state to another. For example, ice will **melt** (or liquify) from solid ice into liquid water at 0°C. This temperature is water's **melting point**. Water will **boil** (or evaporate) into steam at 100°C. This is water's **boiling point**.

These changes can be reversed by cooling down the substance; a gas that gets cold enough **condenses** into a liquid and a liquid **solidifies** into a solid.

Quick change

Some substances, such as moth balls, go straight from being a solid to a gas, without ever becoming a liquid.

This is called **sublimation** and it's why moth balls disappear into thin air, leaving only a smell behind.

How does ice make drinks cold?

What happens when water boils?

Molecules in the air

Air is made up of atoms and molecules of different gases. They're constantly rushing about, bashing into things. This creates something called **air pressure**.

You need air pressure to hold yourself together. Inside your body, blood pumps around and pushes outwards, but air pressure pushes back. It's this balance which stops you from bursting out of your skin.

You don't usually notice air molecules knocking into you. But sometimes they move more quickly than normal. That's what wind is.

Water pressure

Water is heavier than air, so under water there's more pressure than on land.

The deeper you go, the stronger it gets.

Deep sea submarines need incredibly thick hulls to cope with the pressure of the water pushing all around them.

How does pressure affect state?

The amount of pressure on a substance affects how free its molecules are to move around. So changing the pressure can sometimes cause a change of state, even without a change in temperature.

For example, squeezing a gas into a really tight space puts extra pressure on the gas. This can turn some gases into liquids, and make them stay that way.

At very low temperatures nitrogen gas becomes a liquid. This liquid can be stored in a pressurized container to stop its molecules from spreading out and becoming a gas again, even if the container is then kept at room temperature.

When liquid nitrogen is released from the container, at room temperature, it immediately turns back into a gas.

The yellow canister contains liquid nitrogen. As it is poured out, it turns into a gas. To do this, it takes heat from the molecules in the air. In turn, this makes **water vapour** in the air condense into water and this appears as a white mist.

16

How do we know about this?

Gases always spread out to fill whatever space they're in. This makes them really tricky to catch and study. 17th-century Irish chemist Robert Boyle was one of the first people to manage it.

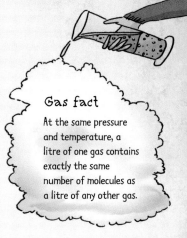

First, he invented a perfectly airtight container he could fill with air (with help from his physicist friend, Robert Hooke). Then, he built a pump that could suck the air back out again. By experimenting with this pump, Boyle discovered he could make a gas take up less space by putting pressure on it – and vice versa.

Gas fact

At the same pressure and temperature, a litre of one gas contains exactly the same number of molecules as a litre of any other gas.

How Boyle made a balloon get bigger – without blowing any extra air into it.

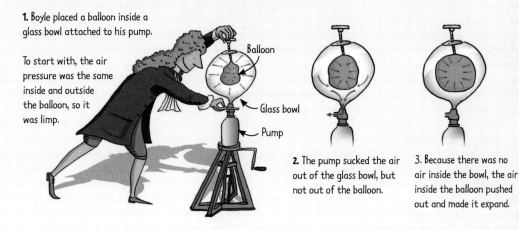

1. Boyle placed a balloon inside a glass bowl attached to his pump.

To start with, the air pressure was the same inside and outside the balloon, so it was limp.

Balloon

Glass bowl

Pump

2. The pump sucked the air out of the glass bowl, but not out of the balloon.

3. Because there was no air inside the bowl, the air inside the balloon pushed out and made it expand.

Boyle used his pump for other experiments, too. He proved that animals need air to breathe, and that candles need air to stay alight. But he never found out what air is made of.

It's actually a mixture of different gases, but most of them weren't discovered until the 20th century. Separating them out was just too difficult.

What's in air?

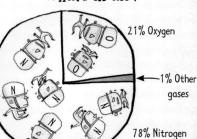

21% Oxygen

1% Other gases

78% Nitrogen

Know your properties

Two hundred years ago, scientists didn't know about different kinds of atoms, or even that atoms existed at all. But early chemists still knew an awful lot about how substances work, and what they can do. This is because they studied what are known as the physical and chemical properties of a susbtance.

What are physical properties?

Physical properties mostly describe what a substance is like on its own. The most basic example is what it looks like. Many physical properties are easy to find out, such as what colour a substance is, what it smells like, or what state it's in at room temperature.

Other physical properties can be found using simple tests. For example, you can heat a liquid to find its **boiling point** (the temperature at which it boils and changes state to become a gas). Or, if it's a solid, you can hit it, to see if it breaks into pieces or buckles, or if it's too strong even to dent.

What are chemical properties?

Chemical properties mostly describe what a substance can do, such as what happens when you heat it up, or mix it with other substances. For example, some things turn a different colour as they burn, or dissolve when mixed with water, or explode when mixed with acid.

The only way to test a chemical property is to make a chemical reaction happen. Creating a reaction is a bit like cooking – chemists do it by mixing together different substances, and often heating them up as well.

Salt facts

White solid; made up of little crystals.

Compound made of the elements sodium and chlorine.

No smell; tastes salty.

Boiling point: 1465°C

Melting point: 801°C

Flaming salt

1. Light a candle.

2. Put a few grains of salt onto a spoon.

3. Pour the salt onto the candle and watch...

...you should see tiny orange sparks appear. This is because sodium, one of the elements in salt, makes an orange flame.

Dissolving things

If you stir sugar into warm water, the sugar disappears. Chemists call this **dissolving**. The sugar and water molecules have mixed together. You might think they've bonded to make a compound, but they haven't. They've become a liquid mixture called a **solution**. The ability to do this is a property of both sugar *and* water.

Another property of water is that the hotter it gets, the easier it becomes to dissolve things in it. This explains why you sometimes find a sticky layer at the bottom of a cup of cold tea. This is sugar that has 'dropped out' of solution as the tea cooled.

The molecules in water and sugar mix together to make a solution.

Oil doesn't dissolve in water. Even if you stir it, it soon floats to the top.

Pure and simple

When a substance contains only one kind of atom or molecule, and is not contaminated by other stuff, chemists describe it as **pure**. One way to see if a sample is pure is by looking at its physical properties.

For example, one physical property of pure water is that it boils at 100°C. If a substance *looks* like water but doesn't boil at this temperature, then either it's not water, or it's not pure. The substances that make a sample *impure* are often called **contaminants** and they change the boiling point.

Tap water is never pure, so if you could measure the temperature of boiling tap water (you'd need a special thermometer from a lab to do this accurately), you'd find it boils at just *over* 100°C. This is because it contains small amounts of chlorine, which has been added to kill any harmful bugs.

Don't forget about pressure!

On top of high mountains, there is less air pressure than on the ground. This means that water can boil at a cooler temperature than normal. But tea made with 'cold' boiled water isn't very tasty...

Yuck!

Sorting out substances

Chemists can use their knowledge of properties to extract pure substances from impure samples. Here are some examples:

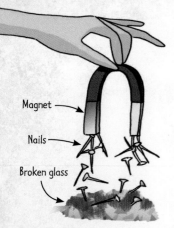

Magnet

Nails

Broken glass

How can you separate steel nails from broken glass?
Use a magnet. The nails will be attracted to the magnet and stick to it, but the glass will not.

How can you separate salt from oil?
Pour the salty oil into a jug of water. The salt will dissolve in the water, but the oil will not. The oil will float on top of the water and can be carefully poured off (or removed using a separating funnel, like the one on the left). The water can then be boiled away to leave behind pure salt.

Special equipment
Separating mixtures is easy with the right equipment. Chemists often make their own glass tubes and bottles to make sure they have exactly what they need.

Separating funnel

Oil

Tap

This separating funnel makes it easy to see and separate two liquids by draining one away from the other.

Flask

Water

How can you separate a mixture of sand and salt?
Add water to the mixture. This dissolves the salt but not the sand. If you pour this through a sheet of **filter paper**, the sand will collect on it, and the salt solution will flow through. This is called **filtration**. Finally, the water can be boiled off, leaving the salt behind.

Filter paper

Mixture of sand and salt water

Funnel

Salt water

Filter paper has tiny holes that are too small to see.

Sand can't fit through the holes...

...but salt water can.

How can you separate a solution?

Solutions can appear tricky to separate because the molecules inside are so mixed up. But a chemist just needs to know the different properties of the substance that's dissolved – called the **solute** – and the liquid it's dissolved in, called the **solvent**.

Separation technique No. 1: Distillation

Distillation is a method of purifying solutions by using boiling points. Usually, the aim is to boil off the solvent, and collect it as a pure liquid.

Heating a solution makes the solvent boil, forming a gas. This leaves behind the solute that was mixed into it. Meanwhile, the hot gas can flow into a long tube. Cold water is passed around the tube. This cools down the gas, until it becomes a liquid again. This liquid is pure and can now be collected.

Distilling fuels

Crude oil is a mixture of fuels and other useful substances. They can all be separated by a technique called fractional distillation, which uses chemists' knowledge of substances' boiling points.

The substances in crude oil have very different boiling points. Natural gas boils off first at 36°C, then petrol at 71°C and finally tar at about 515°C.

This is an example of distillation apparatus.

Do-it-yourself distillation

This experiment shows how to distill pure water from sugar water.

⚠ **WARNING**
Watch out: steam is very hot and can burn.

1. Pour a glass of water into a saucepan, and stir in a spoonful of sugar. It will now taste sugary.

2. Heat the sugar water until it boils. Wearing an oven glove, catch the steam on a metal tray.

3. On the tray, the steam condenses into drops of water. Taste it – it won't be sugary any more.

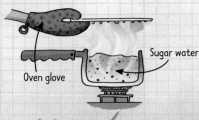

Oven glove

Sugar water

Separation technique No. 2: Chromatography

Chromatography is used to separate mixtures of many substances. There are two types: paper and gas.

Paper chromatography tells scientists what all the different parts of a mixture are. But it doesn't purify them. The mixture to be separated is dissolved in a solvent. The solution is then absorbed along the length of a piece of paper.

The different solutes spread out along the paper. Some spread further than others, depending on how strongly they stick to the paper (that's one of their properties). This piece of paper is known as a **chromatogram**. By studying it, chemists can identify the different substances spread across it.

Gas chromatography is used to help to identify tiny amounts of substances in a mixture. It even works on just a few molecules. Chemists turn the test substance into a gas and feed it into a machine. A computer records how the molecules spread out inside the machine and creates a chromatogram.

Chemists can compare this to chromatograms of known substances, in order to identify the molecules.

A gas chromatography machine uses a liquid or gas (instead of paper) to separate the sample. This means the separated parts can be collected once they've been through the machine. So this method can be used to purify substances as well as to identify them.

A chromatogram from a computer looks like a huge graph. Chemists can find out lots of information from it.

Who developed it?

Me! Mikhail Tsvet. I developed chromatography in 1901 to find out what makes plants green.

Crime solving

Detectives can use chromatography to identify unknown substances at a crime scene, such as poisons or explosives.

Do-it-yourself chromatography

Most felt-tip pens contain a mixture of dyes to make up their colour.
You can separate the dyes yourself, using paper chromatography.

1. Cut a strip of coffee filter paper. Dab ink from some felt-tip pens onto it, just above the bottom.

2. Wind the top of the paper around a pencil, stick it in place, and hang it inside a glass with a little water.

3. Leave it for a few minutes. Each ink should spread up the paper, separating into its different dyes.

Filter paper

Ink spots

The bottom of the paper should just touch the water. The water doesn't need to touch the ink spots.

A chromatogram of inks

Separation technique No. 3: Centrifugation

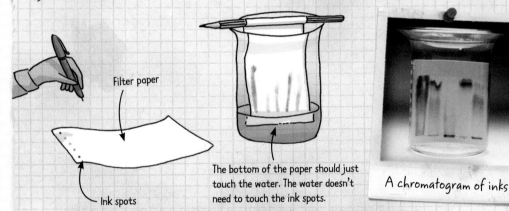

Centrifugation uses a machine called a **centrifuge** to separate solutions into liquids that have different densities. **Density** is the amount of **mass**, or stuff, in a certain **volume**, or space. Things that aren't very dense will float on top of denser things. For example, oil is less dense than water, so oil floats on water.

The solution is placed in a set of test tubes and clipped to the centrifuge. It spins around really, really fast, forcing the denser parts to settle at the bottom of each tube. If the solution also contains any solid bits, they will sink to the very bottom.

Blood science

Sports officials often use centrifugation to check blood samples. It can reveal if an athlete has taken any illegal drugs.

23

Rocky reactions

Bauxite is a rocky mixture of compounds that miners dig out of the ground.

In a factory, technicians perform a series of chemical reactions, called the Bayer process, to extract a useful metal, aluminium.

This process leaves behind bits of waste rock and some waste gases.

What's electrolysis useful for?

Electrolysis can be used to coat things in metal. It is commonly used to cover iron objects, such as nails, in zinc to stop them from rusting. This process is called **galvanization**.

Sorting out compounds

Compounds are trickier to separate than mixtures. To get at the elements in them doesn't just mean separating one kind of molecule from another – it means splitting each molecule into separate atoms.

Compounds are created by chemical reactions, so one way to split them is to trigger another reaction. For example, chemists can get copper out of the rocky compound copper oxide by heating the rock with carbon. The carbon swaps places with the copper, leaving behind carbon dioxide and pure copper.

Separation technique No.4: Electrolysis

Some compounds can be split apart using electricity. The compound is either melted or dissolved in a solvent to make something called an **electrolyte**. Then an electric current is passed through it, making the compound break apart. This is called **electrolysis**.

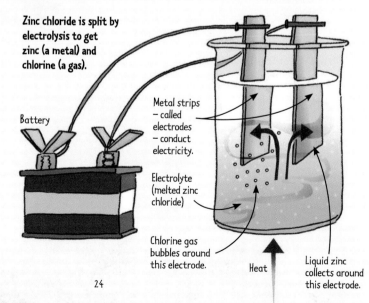

Zinc chloride is split by electrolysis to get zinc (a metal) and chlorine (a gas).

Battery

Metal strips – called electrodes – conduct electricity.

Electrolyte (melted zinc chloride)

Chlorine gas bubbles around this electrode.

Heat

Liquid zinc collects around this electrode.

The story so far

What is the world made of? Here are some of the ways a chemist might answer that question...

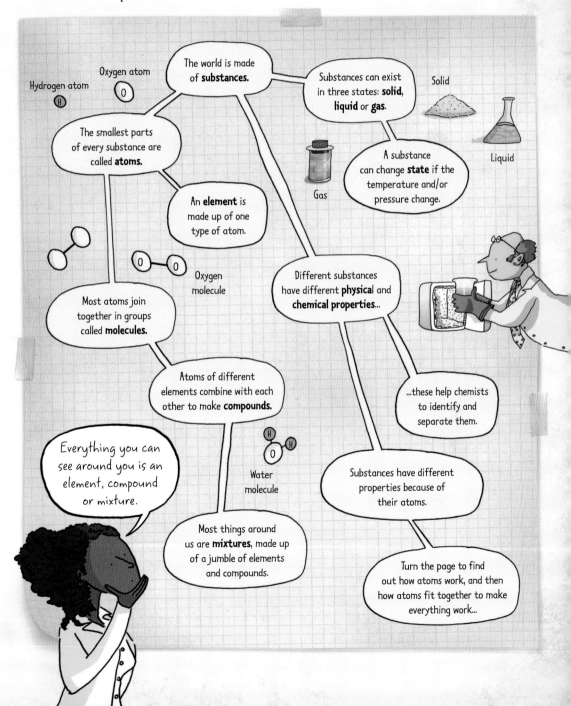

Hydrogen atom

Oxygen atom

The world is made of **substances.**

The smallest parts of every substance are called **atoms.**

An **element** is made up of one type of atom.

Substances can exist in three states: **solid, liquid** or **gas.**

Solid

Liquid

Gas

A substance can change **state** if the temperature and/or pressure change.

Oxygen molecule

Most atoms join together in groups called **molecules.**

Atoms of different elements combine with each other to make **compounds.**

Different substances have different **physical** and **chemical properties...**

...these help chemists to identify and separate them.

Water molecule

Everything you can see around you is an element, compound or mixture.

Most things around us are **mixtures,** made up of a jumble of elements and compounds.

Substances have different properties because of their atoms.

Turn the page to find out how atoms work, and then how atoms fit together to make everything work...

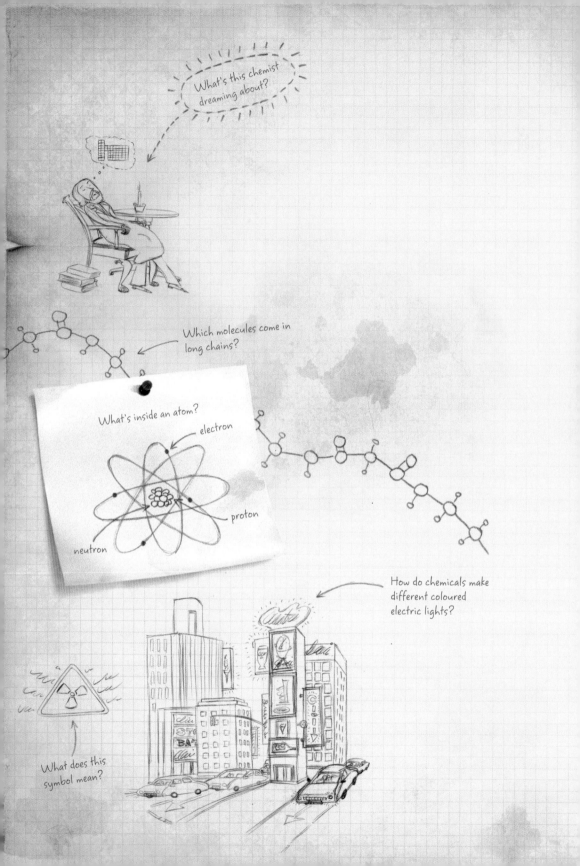

Part 2:
How does it all work?

The big secret behind chemistry is atoms. The reason substances look different and have different properties is all to do with the atoms they're made of. And the reason that chemical reactions happen between substances is to do with the bits inside each of those atoms.

An atom's bits

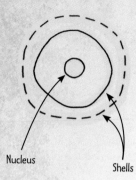

Nucleus

Shells

Feeling electrons

Step 1. Blow up a balloon and rub it on a carpet.

Step 2. Hold the balloon up to your head, and you should find that it'll stick to your hair.

What's going on?
Rubbing the balloon brings lots of electrons to the surface. This gives it a tiny negative electrical charge, which makes the balloon stick to your hair. This is called 'static electricity'.

What's inside an atom?

In the middle of every atom is a central part called the **nucleus**. It contains unimaginably tiny particles called **protons** and **neutrons**, which are all the same size as each other. Most of the rest of an atom is empty space – but at the edge there are even tinier particles called **electrons**, which whizz around the nucleus in layers. These layers are called **shells**. Small atoms only have one shell, but larger atoms can have several.

Protons and electrons both have an **electrical charge**, and it's this charge which holds an atom together. Protons have a positive charge, while electrons have a negative one. (Neutrons have no charge.) When the charges are balanced, they cancel each other out. Atoms have the same number of protons as electrons so, overall, atoms have no charge.

How to identify an atom

Scientists can identify each element by looking for one simple clue: the number of protons in its atoms. For example, an atom with just one proton is a hydrogen atom. An atom with six protons is a carbon atom.

Hydrogen atom

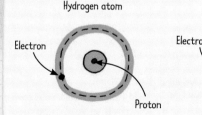

Electron

Proton

Carbon atom

Proton

Electron

Neutron

Hydrogen atoms are unusual – they don't have any neutrons. All other atoms do – usually around the same number as they have protons.

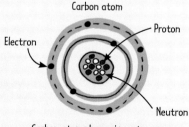

Carbon atoms have six protons and six neutrons inside the nucleus. They also have six electrons in two shells.

Build your own carbon atom

Chemists often make models of atoms to understand how they are put together. You can make your own simple models using grapes, peas, food wrap and cocktail sticks. Here's a model of a carbon atom:

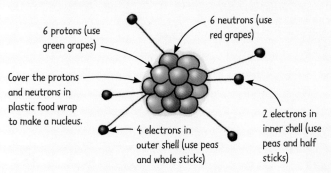

6 protons (use green grapes)

6 neutrons (use red grapes)

Cover the protons and neutrons in plastic food wrap to make a nucleus.

4 electrons in outer shell (use peas and whole sticks)

2 electrons in inner shell (use peas and half sticks)

Naming substances

Scientists often use symbols to describe substances. Oxygen, for example, is O_2. The 'O' is the chemical symbol for oxygen. The '2' (which is always written lower down and a bit smaller) means that one oxygen molecule contains two oxygen atoms.

Compounds get their names by combining the names of the elements in them. For example, carbon dioxide is CO_2. This means it's made of one carbon atom (C) and two oxygen atoms (O_2). $CaCl_2$ is calcium chloride – one atom of calcium (Ca) and two of chlorine (Cl_2).

Luckily, you don't have to memorize the name and symbol of every element. You can look them up – and find out many other things – on a chart called the **Periodic Table**. Turn the page to find out more...

All the atoms

The chart on the next page shows how many protons, neutrons and electrons every atom has.

You can make a model of any atom on the chart – as long as you can find enough fruit.

Symbols

The symbol for many elements is just the first letter of their name:

O = oxygen; **C** = carbon

Some use two letters (the first letter is always a capital):

Mn = manganese; **He** = helium

And some use letters from their name in Latin or Arabic:

K = potassium (Arabic: kalium)

Fe = iron (Latin: ferrum)

All chemicals have formal, scientific names, but lots of them have common names, too. For example, 'dihydrogen oxide' is better known as plain old 'water'.

Ah, nice cool dihydrogen oxide!

The Periodic Table

The Periodic Table lists all the elements in order of their **atomic number** (the number of protons in one atom). The table is divided into rows, called **periods,** and columns. Eight of the columns are called **groups**.

Elements in the same group have the same number of electrons in their outermost shell. Elements in the same period have the same number of shells. You can find out why shells are so important on page 35.

What's in each box?

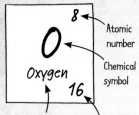

8 — Atomic number

O

Oxygen

16

Chemical symbol

Name of element   Mass number

The **atomic number** is the number of protons.

The **mass number** is the number of protons plus the number of neutrons.

It's called the 'mass' number because it also shows the amount of stuff (or mass) in each atom. Electrons are so small – they have just $1/1800^{th}$ the mass of a proton or neutron – that they hardly have any mass at all.

Who came up with the Periodic Table?

Lots of people tried to draw up a table of elements, but the first person to make it work was Russian chemist Dmitri Mendeleev in 1869. He said the idea for it came to him in a dream.

Types of elements

Hydrogen is a type all on its own.

Very reactive metals (see page 32)

Quite reactive metals (see page 32)

Transition metals (see page 32)

Poor metals (see page 32)

Metalloids (see page 33)

Non metals (see page 33)

Noble gases (see page 33)

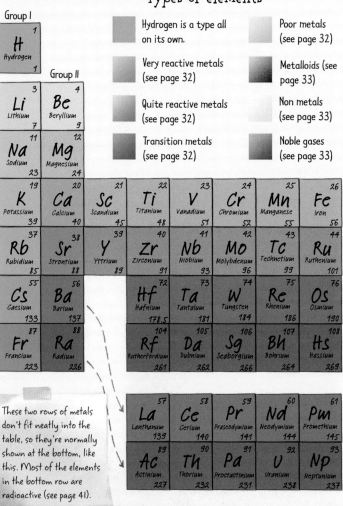

Group I

1
H
Hydrogen
1

Group II

3	4
Li	Be
Lithium	Beryllium
7	9

11	12
Na	Mg
Sodium	Magnesium
23	24

19	20	21	22	23	24	25	26
K	Ca	Sc	Ti	V	Cr	Mn	Fe
Potassium	Calcium	Scandium	Titanium	Vanadium	Chromium	Manganese	Iron
39	40	45	48	51	52	55	56

37	38	39	40	41	42	43	44
Rb	Sr	Y	Zr	Nb	Mo	Tc	Ru
Rubidium	Strontium	Yttrium	Zirconium	Niobium	Molybdenum	Technetium	Ruthenium
85	88	89	91	93	96	99	101

55	56	72	73	74	75	76
Cs	Ba	Hf	Ta	W	Re	Os
Caesium	Barium	Hafnium	Tantalum	Tungsten	Rhenium	Osmium
133	137	178.5	181	184	186	190

87	88	104	105	106	107	108
Fr	Ra	Rf	Da	Sg	Bh	Hs
Francium	Radium	Rutherfordium	Dubnium	Seaborgium	Bohrium	Hassium
223	226	261	262	266	264	269

These two rows of metals don't fit neatly into the table, so they're normally shown at the bottom, like this. Most of the elements in the bottom row are radioactive (see page 41).

57	58	59	60	61
La	Ce	Pr	Nd	Pm
Lanthanum	Cerium	Praseodymium	Neodymium	Promethium
139	140	141	144	145

89	90	91	92	93
Ac	Th	Pa	U	Np
Actinium	Thorium	Proactinium	Uranium	Neptunium
227	232	231	238	237

If you know a bit about the properties of just a few elements you can use this table to work out what properties other elements nearby might have, and which elements they're likely to react with.

The table is still growing. Only the elements up to number 93 are naturally occuring; all the higher elements have been artificially created in labs. So far no one has managed to make any of element number 117 – that's why there's a gap on the table.

Periods

Going across the periods from left to right, atoms increase in mass, because they contain more bits.

Surprisingly, they also get smaller, because the increasing electrical charge pulls the bits closer together.

Groups

Elements in the same group usually have similar properties. Going down the groups from top to bottom, atoms get bigger. They also tend to have lower melting points and are generally easier to break apart.

				Group III	Group IV	Group V	Group VI	Group VII	Group VIII
									2 He Helium 4
				5 B Boron 11	6 C Carbon 12	7 N Nitrogen 14	8 O Oxygen 16	9 F Fluorine 19	10 Ne Neon 20
				13 Al Aluminium 27	14 Si Silicon 28	15 P Phosphorus 31	16 S Sulphur 32	17 Cl Chlorine 35.5	18 Ar Argon 40
27 Co Cobalt 59	28 Ni Nickel 59	29 Cu Copper 64	30 Zn Zinc 65	31 Ga Gallium 70	32 Ge Germanium 73	33 As Arsenic 75	34 Se Selenium 79	35 Br Bromine 79	36 Kr Krypton 84
45 Rh Rhodium 103	46 Pd Palladium 106	47 Ag Silver 108	48 Cd Cadmium 112	49 In Indium 115	50 Sn Tin 119	51 Sb Antimony 122	52 Te Tellurium 128	53 I Iodine 127	54 Xe Xenon 131
77 Ir Iridium 192	78 Pt Platinum 195	79 Au Gold 197	80 Hg Mercury 201	81 Ti Thallium 204	82 Pb Lead 207	83 Bi Bismuth 209			86 Rn Radon 222
109 Mt Meitnerium 268	110 Ds Darmstadtium 271	111 Rg Roentgenium 272	112 Uub Ununbium 277	113 Uut Ununtrium 284	114 Uuq Ununquadium 289	115 Uup Ununpentium 288	116 Uuh Ununhexium 293		

62 Sm Samarium 150	63 Eu Europium 152	64 Gd Gadolinium 157	65 Tb Terbium 159	66 Dy Dysprosium 163	67 Ho Holmium 165	68 Er Erbium 167	69 Tm Thulium 169	70 Yb Ytterbium 173	71 Lu Lutetium 268
94 Pu Plutonium 244	95 Am Americium 243	96 Cm Curium 247	97 Bk Berkelium 247	98 Cf Californium 251	99 Es Einsteinium 252	100 Fm Fermium 257	101 Md Meitnerium 258	102 No Nobelium 259	103 Lr Lawrencium 262

Metals

Most elements are **metals**. The easiest way to identify a metal is how it looks. All pure metals are shiny, and they share many other properties, too. Here are some of them...

Metals can be drawn out into wires, and are good at conducting electricity (see page 38).

PIIIING!!!

When solid, metals make a pinging sound if they're hit.

Metals can be bent without breaking.

Reactive metals

The elements in Groups I and II are all reactive metals. Because of this, they can be hard to find in their pure forms.

Two of the reactive metals in Group I, sodium and potassium, are so reactive that they catch fire when they come into contact with water.

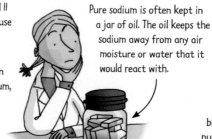

Pure sodium is often kept in a jar of oil. The oil keeps the sodium away from any air moisture or water that it would react with.

Transition metals

Transition metals make up a large block of elements. Many can be found in pure form, but they can also be combined to create metallic mixtures called alloys (see page 67). Transition metals include iron, copper, zinc, cobalt and mercury.

Poor metals

Most of the elements in Groups III-VI are metals, but many are softer and easier to melt than other metals. This makes them useful for different things. Common examples include aluminium, tin and lead.

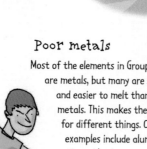

Most drinks cans are made of aluminium. It's a soft metal that's easy to crush.

Elements, such as zinc and cobalt, are used to make the colours in stained glass.

32

Metalloids

Seven elements in Groups III-VI share some properties with metals, and some with non-metals. These in-betweeners are known as **metalloids**.

Silicon microchip

Circuit board

The metalloid silicon can conduct electricity, but only when it's heated up. Substances that do this are called **semi-conductors**.

Microchips are often made of silicon and are used on circuit boards. They turn on a circuit when heated up, and turn it off again when they're cooled down.

Non metals

Unlike metals, all **non metals** don't conduct heat or electricity very well at all. Many of them are gases at room temperature.

There are only 16 non metals, but they make up much of the world around us – including the atmosphere, the oceans and much of the Earth's crust.

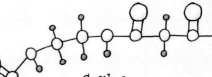

Carbon

One non metal that is particularly interesting to chemists is carbon (see pages 64-65). It's such a useful element that there's a whole branch of chemistry, called '**organic chemistry**', devoted to it.

This diagram shows a carbon-based, chain-like molecule which is used to make plastics.

Sulphur

At room temperature, sulphur is a brittle yellow block that crumbles easily. It's used to make gunpowder and match heads.

Noble gases

Noble gases are incredibly unreactive non metals. Four of them share one very useful property – they produce a coloured light when an electric current passes through them.

Noble gases are used to light up cities at night.

What colour?

Neon makes red or orange lights.

Argon with mercury makes blue lights.

Krypton lights are pale pink.

Xenon lights are purple.

Safe storage

Nitrogen is often used inside food packets. It keeps out oxygen, which would make the food go stale.

Pure krypton is used as part of really powerful lasers, for example in eye surgery.

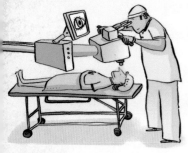

Complex compounds

Some compounds are made up of lots and lots of different atoms. In 1945, British chemist Dorothy Crowfoot Hodgkin worked out the complex structure of the compound that makes the drug penicillin.

Pure elements

Only a few elements are found and used in their pure forms. For example, very unreactive elements such as gold, or the noble gases, almost always occur as pure elements. Some elements, such as copper, are often found in their pure forms because they are only reactive under certain conditions. Others, such as carbon, react quite easily, but they can exist on their own, too.

Other substances are found as elements because they're in plentiful supply. Oxygen and nitrogen are both reactive gases, but there's so much of them in the air that they couldn't possibly find enough other substances to react with.

People and animals inhale oxygen all day, every day, but more is constantly being produced by plants. So the supply of fresh oxygen never runs out.

How are compounds made?

Most substances aren't elements — they're compounds or mixtures. The reason compounds exist is all to do with the electrons in a substance's atoms.

When two or more atoms collide, they may just bounce off each other. But sometimes, a few electrons are transferred from one atom to another. This changes the atoms, and makes them bond together. That's how compounds are made.

This process is called a chemical reaction, and it happens because of the number of electrons the atoms have in their outer shells.

How do shells work?

The first shell around a nucleus only has room for two electrons. The second and higher shells each have room for eight. When the first shell is full, a second shell forms. When the second shell is full, a third forms – and so on. The outer shells of the biggest atoms can fit as many as 32 electrons.

The key to chemical reactions is that atoms are much less likely to react if their outer shell is full. Or, to put it another way, most atoms want to be stable, so they try to find ways to have full outer shells.

For example, a hydrogen atom has one electron in its outer shell; but a helium atom has two. Helium is a stable element that hardly ever reacts. But hydrogen is very reactive, because it's always trying to fill its shell.

A hydrogen atom has room for another electron in its shell.

A helium atom has a full outer shell.

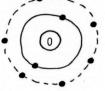

An oxygen atom has six electrons in its outer shell – so it 'wants' two more.

Going around

Electrons don't really travel around in neat, round shells. It's just easier to draw them that way.

In reality, chemists think electrons probably move in cloud shapes, a bit like this:

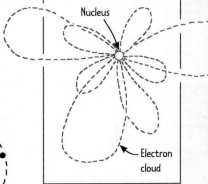

Nucleus

Electron cloud

Gaining and losing

Not all atoms want to *add* more electrons to fill their shells. Some have nearly empty outer shells with one, two or three 'spare' electrons that they want to *lose*.

An atom of lithium, for example, has three electrons: two in its inner shell, and one in its outer shell. Instead of trying to find seven extra electrons, it's easier to lose one electron – leaving it with a single, full shell.

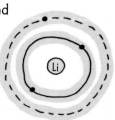

Half full

Transition metals have outer shells that are half full (or half empty). They are happy to add *or* give away electrons.

This means their properties are less predictable than other groups of elements. Some of them are really reactive and others can be very stable and unreactive.

No reactions

Helium   Neon   Argon

Krypton   Xenon   Radon

Remember it's very difficult to make noble gases react with anything. That's because their outer shells are already full and they aren't interested in gaining or losing any electrons.

How do atoms fill up their shells?

In a chemical reaction, atoms can either give or take electrons, or they can share them.

This works in three different ways...

1. Giving and taking electrons

Some atoms need to get rid of just one or two electrons to get a full outer shell. But they can't simply release their electrons into thin air – they have to find other atoms that need electrons. Then there's a bit of give and take, which chemists call **ionic bonding**.

Here's how it works when an atom of sodium meets an atom of chlorine...

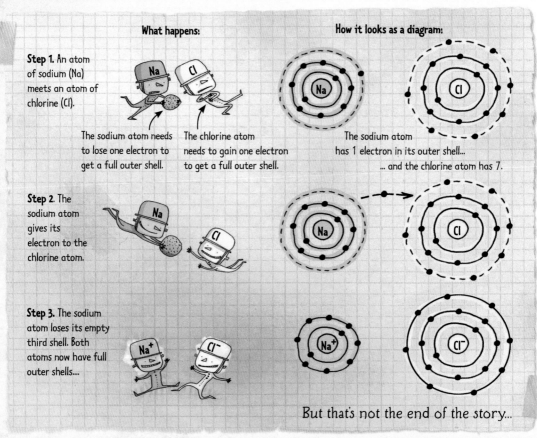

What happens:

Step 1. An atom of sodium (Na) meets an atom of chlorine (Cl).

The sodium atom needs to lose one electron to get a full outer shell.

The chlorine atom needs to gain one electron to get a full outer shell.

Step 2. The sodium atom gives its electron to the chlorine atom.

Step 3. The sodium atom loses its empty third shell. Both atoms now have full outer shells....

How it looks as a diagram:

The sodium atom has 1 electron in its outer shell...

... and the chlorine atom has 7.

But that's not the end of the story...

After giving or taking electrons, an atom has an unequal number of electrons and protons. This gives it an electrical charge. Atoms with a charge are called **ions**. Electrons have a negative charge, so an atom that has gained electrons becomes a **negative ion**. An atom that has lost electrons becomes a **positive ion**.

Ions with opposite charges attract each other. After sodium and chlorine atoms have reacted and become ions, millions of them stick together to make structures that are big enough to see with your naked eye — chemists call these **crystals**.

2. Sharing electrons

Some atoms bond by sharing electrons. They do this by overlapping their outer shells. The shared electrons sit between the atoms, giving them both full outer shells. Chemists call this **covalent bonding**.

Here's how it works for two hydrogen atoms...

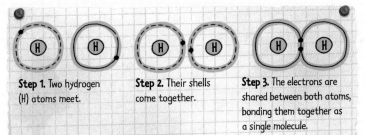

Step 1. Two hydrogen (H) atoms meet.

Step 2. Their shells come together.

Step 3. The electrons are shared between both atoms, bonding them together as a single molecule.

Atoms that have formed covalent bonds usually make small molecules. These molecules don't attract each other very much, because they have no charge. Instead they're free to spread out. That's why many elements and compounds made of covalent bonds, including hydrogen, are gases at room temperature.

Ionic bonds

Na^+ is the symbol for a sodium ion (positive charge).

Cl^- is the symbol for a chlorine ion (negative charge).

Millions of ions of sodium and chlorine bond to make crystals of a stable compound called sodium chloride — better known as table salt.

Covalent bonds

In a hydrogen molecule, two hydrogen atoms share one pair of electrons. This forms a bond called a single bond.

Some molecules, such as carbon monoxide, share two pairs of electrons. This makes a double bond, drawn like this:

Methyl-acrylonitirile is a compound made of 10 atoms. Each molecule contains seven single bonds, one double bond and one triple bond.

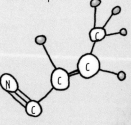

Making magnets

The way that electrons pool in some metals, such as iron, gives them a special property – it makes them magnetic.

3. Pooling electrons

Metal atoms have another way of sharing electrons: they cluster together and pool some of their outer electrons into a sort of sea that floats around them.

Electrons in this sea can flow around any of the atoms that are nearby, so every atom feels as if it has a full outer shell. Because all the metal atoms release some electrons, they all become positive ions.

— Electron

— Metal ion

The electrons in the 'sea' are free to move around and join up with different shells.

Heat race

Here's a quick experiment you can try to test how well metals can conduct heat compared to non metals:

First, make a nice, hot cup of tea. Then, take two spoons made of different material – one metal, the other plastic.

Stick them into the hot tea. Then stick both spoons into a glass full of ice cubes.

You will find that the metal spoon gets hot and cools down much quicker than the plastic spoon.

Explaining metals

Metal atoms cluster together in a regular pattern which chemists call a **giant metallic lattice**. In a metallic lattice, the atoms are packed together very tightly. This makes them extremely hard and is why they have very high boiling points and are solid at room temperature.

The sea of electrons around the lattice creates some useful effects. Electrons can carry heat and electrical energy. Because each electron can move around freely, it's easy for it to knock into and transfer energy to the other electrons next to it. This means heat or an electric current can flow through a metal very quickly. Because of this ability, chemists describe metals as being good **conductors**.

Sticking together

Most individual molecules and ions are too small to see. But the way they stick together affects how different substances look and behave.

Crystals of magnesium sulphate (epsom salt)

How do ions stick together?

Ions nearly always stick together to make crystals. These always have a regular pattern – imagine it as a bit like a climbing frame. The ions are the joints, and the bonds are the bars. The more ions that cluster together, the larger the crystal. Individual crystals can grow quite big. On the next page, you can find out how to grow your own.

It's usually very difficult to pull ions apart physically – even if you heat them up – so most **ionic compounds** are solid even at very high temperatures. But you can break whole *layers* of crystals apart from each other. This is how you can crumble salt into your food. You're not breaking apart the ions in the salt, but you're breaking apart salt crystals.

Inside sodium chloride, ions of sodium and chlorine bond together in a regular pattern.

How do molecules stick together?

Molecules with covalent bonds form **covalent compounds**. There is still an attraction between the individual molecules, but it's weak. So weak, in fact, that these compounds are usually liquids or gases.

For example, water molecules only stick together quite loosely, which is why water is liquid at room temperature. Many gases, including oxygen and nitrogen, are made of covalent molecules, too.

Dissolving ions

Ionic bonds can be broken apart chemically, just by mixing them with the right substance.

For example, salt (sodium chloride) ions will separate when they mix with water. That's what's happening when salt dissolves. But no reaction has happened, so salt water is a mixture, not a compound.

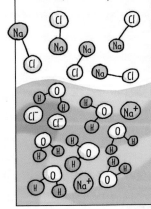

Do-it-yourself crystals

You can grow your own crystals using bicarbonate of soda ($NaHCO_3$). This experiment shows you how.

1. Fill two jars with hot water. Stir about six teaspoons of bicarbonate of soda into each jar. Keep adding more soda until no more will dissolve.

2. Put the jars in a warm place with a plate in between them. Make sure they won't get moved.

3. Cut a piece of wool as long as your arm. Tie a paperclip to each end of it, and place one end in each jar.

4. Leave the jars for at least a week. Crystals should grow gradually along the wool, and hang down over the plate.

what's happening?

Bicarbonate of soda is usually sold as a powder made up of tiny crystals. The powder dissolves in water. The mixture of water and soda is soaked up by the wool. The water then evaporates slowly, leaving behind pure bicarbonate of soda – which reforms into big crystals.

Nuclear reactions

Radiation

Not all reactions happen because of electrons. Sometimes, the nucleus of an atom can split apart by itself, or fuse with the nucleus of another atom. These are both called **nuclear reactions**.

Nuclear reactions change one kind of element into another, because protons are lost or added. But they're pretty rare because they need lots of energy. They usually only happen inside stars, or power generators called nuclear reactors.

This symbol means a substance is radioactive (see below) and will emit radiation. Radiation is dangerous because it can cause serious illnesses, including cancer.

Unstable elements

A few elements have an unstable mix of protons and neutrons in their atoms. Because of this, the nucleus in any of these atoms can suddenly break down and emit (send out) some of its bits. Scientists call these unstable elements **radioactive**. The stuff they emit is called **radiation**.

Uranium is one of the few radioactive elements that can be dug out of the ground. It's found in lumps of rock called pitchblende. Inside pitchblende, single atoms of uranium emit two protons and two neutrons. These fuse to make something called an **alpha particle**. Losing these particles converts the uranium atom into a thorium atom.

Who discovered radioactivity?

I did - Henri Becquerel. I found that uranium salts have strange properties.

What about me - Marie Curie? My husband and I discovered radioactive elements in pitchblende. We invented the word 'radioactivity'.

The Curies and Becquerel shared a Nobel Prize for their work in 1903.

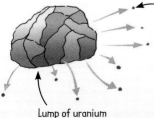

Alpha particle

By the time all the atoms inside a lump of uranium have emitted alpha particles, it has become a lump of thorium.

Lump of uranium

A brief history of atoms

Some of the first people to hit on the idea of atom-like particles were scholars in India about 2,700 years ago.

An Ancient Greek philosopher called Democritus invented the word 'atom' about 2,500 years ago. He had the idea that substances could be divided into smaller and smaller parts, until you found a particle so tiny it couldn't be divided any more. He called these particles 'atoms', which means 'uncuttable' in Ancient Greek.

The idea of atoms was ignored for centuries, because scientists were more interested in studying whole substances. Then, in the 18th century, Amedeo Avogadro in Italy began to study the way gases take up more or less space when temperature and pressure change. He guessed this happens because gases are made of tiny moving parts.

Amedeo Avogadro

In 1803, English chemist John Dalton was investigating how reactions work. He suggested that every element and compound must be made of minuscule particles, and he reused Democritus's word – atom. Over the next hundred years, scientists came to believe that atoms must really exist.

Ernest Rutherford won a Nobel prize in 1908 for his study of radioactivity.

After the discovery of radiation in the 19th century, scientists began to realize that supposedly 'uncuttable' atoms were actually made up of even smaller parts. In 1909, New Zealander Ernest Rutherford used radiation to detect the nucleus of a gold atom.

In 1913, Danish scientist Niels Bohr suggested a way that electrons could fit around an atom's nucleus. This finally explained how atoms react with each other.

Niels Bohr

Atoms and bonds: need to know

An atom

Atoms are made of protons, neutrons and electrons.

Protons and neutrons stick together in the atom's nucleus.

Electrons orbit around the atom in layers called shells.

Protons and electrons have opposite charges, so they attract each other. Atoms have the same number of electrons as protons.

Nucleus

Shell

This diagram shows four electron shells circling the nucleus from different angles.

Proton (+)

The number of protons tells you what element an atom belongs to.

Electron (−)

Neutron (no charge)

Atoms are more stable if their outer shell is full of electrons. If they don't have a full shell, they will react with other atoms until they do. They can do this in three ways:

3. Metal atoms join together in a giant metallic lattice, pooling their electrons in a sea that flows all around them.

1. Some atoms give or take electrons to become ions.

Ions have a positive or negative charge. Opposite ions attract each other and make ionic compounds.

2. Some atoms overlap their shells, and share their electrons to become molecules.

Part 3:
Let's make things happen!

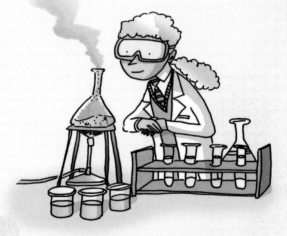

Chemistry can sometimes seem like magic.
After all, how on earth does a firework explode into
different coloured lights when you set it off? And how
can a dangerous acid turn into harmless and tasty table
salt? What's really going on (in both cases) is just a
chemical reaction. But the effects of any reaction can be
spectacular, surprising – and often very useful...

Reactions: the basics

Reactions happen between the *atoms* of different substances but the results affect the *whole* substances.

Substances that react are called **reactants**, and any new substances formed by the reaction are called **products**. Reactions also take in and give out **energy** – usually as heat or light (for example, as a flame). But this energy doesn't count as a reactant or a product.

When reactants are mixed together, most of their molecules or ions will react, if part of one reactant is attracted to part of another. Their molecules break down, and rearrange to form new products. But there can be some molecules of each reactant that don't react, so they're left over at the end.

Reactions all around

Chemical reactions are happening all around us, all the time. They're even happening inside your body right now. When you breathe in air, the oxygen it contains reacts with chemicals from your food, producing carbon dioxide and water vapour (which you breathe out). This reaction also gives out energy, providing power for your cells, organs, muscles and brain.

By-products

Chemists often use a reaction to get a specific product. Any other products are then described as **by-products**. Many by-products are useful, but some are dangerous – such as polluting smoke that comes from coal-burning power stations.

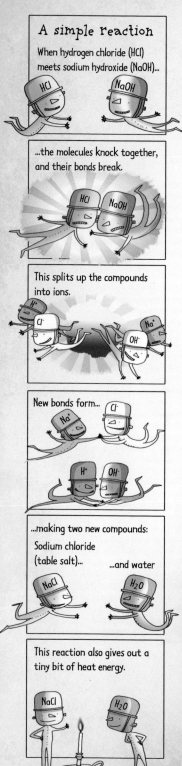

A simple reaction

When hydrogen chloride (HCl) meets sodium hydroxide (NaOH)...

...the molecules knock together, and their bonds break.

This splits up the compounds into ions.

New bonds form...

...making two new compounds:
Sodium chloride (table salt)...   ...and water

This reaction also gives out a tiny bit of heat energy.

How do reactions start?

No matter how keen a substance is to react, a certain amount of energy is needed to kick-start any reaction. That's because energy is needed to help break the existing bonds inside the reactants.

Energy to start a reaction can come in different forms. Most often it's heat, but it could also be light or electricity. And some energy (again, usually heat) is given out at the end when the products are formed.

Heat in, heat out

Some reactions take in more heat at the start than they give out at the end. These are called **endothermic** reactions. For example, when you eat sherbet, it takes heat from your body to react with water in your mouth. This makes your tongue tingle (it's really feeling cold).

Exothermic reactions are the opposite — they give out more than they take in. If you drop an indigestion tablet into a bowl of vinegar, it will fizz. The bowl becomes warm, because the reaction gives out heat.

Food chemistry

Baking and cooking are just chemical reactions in a kitchen. Heating food speeds up the reaction between the ingredients. Stirring helps the ingredients (or reactants) to mix together properly, so they react more swiftly.

Yum!

Lunching on light

Plants use the green stuff in their leaves (called chlorophyll) to capture light energy from sunshine. This kick-starts a reaction between water and carbon dioxide to make glucose (food). This whole process is called photosynthesis.

Natural torch

Inside a firefly, there's a substance that reacts with oxygen to give out light. This is what makes the firefly glow.

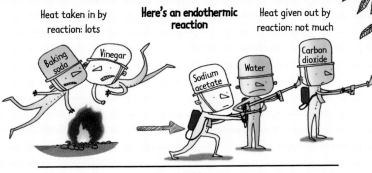

Heat taken in by reaction: lots

Here's an endothermic reaction

Heat given out by reaction: not much

Baking soda · Vinegar · Sodium acetate · Water · Carbon dioxide

Heat taken in by reaction: not much

Here's an exothermic reaction

Heat given out by reaction: lots

Methane · Oxygen · Carbon dioxide · Water

Gunpowder is made of reactants that react so quickly they cause an explosion.

BANG!

Silver objects react with air to form a layer of tarnish. It can be removed by polishing.

Ready, steady, react!

The amount of energy a reaction needs to get going is called its **activation energy**. Some reactions need a lot of activation energy, but others only need a little.

Once they get going, some reactions happen in seconds, such as exploding gunpowder. Others, such as silver turning black (tarnishing), can take many weeks. The rate of a reaction depends on the **reactivity** of the reactants – which means how keen they are to break up and form new products.

Speeding up and slowing down

Many reactions will happen more quickly if you add an extra substance called a **catalyst**. The catalyst isn't a reactant – it just lowers the activation energy. At the end of the reaction, the catalyst is unchanged and can even be used again. Different substances can be catalysts for different reactions. For example, platinum speeds up a reaction in car exhaust pipes to get rid of poisonous gas.

You can slow down or even stop a reaction from happening by adding another susbtance called an **inhibitor**. For example, galvanized iron is coated in a layer of zinc, which is an inhibitor. It slows the reaction between iron and air that forms rust.

Life savers

Your body is brimming with biological catalysts called enzymes. They speed up vital processes that keep you alive.

But sometimes an enzyme can speed up a reaction so much it makes you feel ill or in pain. Many medicines, for example aspirin, work by inhibiting these reactions.

React faster!

Slow down!

Enzyme

Aspirin

Reactions can also be speeded up or slowed down by changing the temperature. Heat makes molecules rush around and collide more often, so they react faster.

But if reactants are cooled down, they have less energy to move around and bash into each other, so they react more slowly.

What's the point of catalysts?

Chemists often do experiments to work out a reaction's activation energy, and which catalysts can help. This is so that they can change the reaction conditions in factories, to manufacture products more quickly and efficiently.

For example, in 1909, German chemist Fritz Haber worked out how to make nitrogen react with hydrogen to produce ammonia (NH_3). This is a key ingredient in many fertilizers, used to help grow crops. Haber found he could produce lots of ammonia by raising the temperature and pressure to the right levels, and adding iron as a catalyst.

Feed the world

Over one third of the world's population relies on food grown with the help of ammonia fertilizers.

Do-it-yourself reaction race

In this simple experiment, you can see for yourself how heat changes the speed of a reaction. You will need some tap water and two soluble indigestion tablets.

1. Take two glasses. Put cold water in the first and hot water in the second.

2. Drop one tablet into each of the glasses at the same time. If you don't drop them in at the same time, it won't be a fair experiment.

Cold water (from the fridge)

Hand-hot water (from the hot tap)

What's going on?

The reaction between the tablets and the water needs a little heat to start. Cold water won't start to fizz until it warms to room temperature. But the hot water kick-starts the reaction right away. This reaction is also exothermic — so when the reactants do start to fizz, they make the water even hotter.

3. Watch the two glasses closely. You should find that the glass with warm water starts to fizz up after a few seconds, before the glass with cold water.

writing down reactions

Chemists write down reactions using **equations** that look a bit like maths. They add the reactants together on the left, then draw an arrow, and finally show what the products are on the right.

Science symbols

Some equations use symbols to give extra information:

⤵ means light energy.

△ means heat energy.

(s), (l) or (g) means a substance is solid, liquid or gas.
(aq) means a substance is 'aqueous' – dissolved in water.

Here's a simple chemical equation in words:

Sodium hydroxide + Hydrochloric acid ⟶ Table salt + Water

And here's how it looks using chemical symbols:

$NaOH + HCl ⟶ NaCl + H_2O$

Balancing equations

One of the most important things to know about reactions is that, overall, nothing is destroyed or made. This is called the **Law of Conservation of Mass**.
It means the total number of atoms of each element has to be the same on both sides of the arrow. This is called balancing the equation.

I'll give this plant sunlight and water so it can make food.

This equation shows the reaction plants use to make glucose (food):

Water + Carbon dioxide $\xrightarrow{\text{+ sunlight}}$ Glucose + Oxygen

Here's how it looks when balanced, using chemical symbols:

$$6H_2O + 6CO_2 \xrightarrow{} C_6H_{12}O_6 + 6O_2$$

There are the same number of carbon, hydrogen and oxygen atoms on both sides of the equation.

On the left:

There are six molecules of water and six molecules of carbon dioxide.

$6 \times H_2 = 12$ hydrogen atoms

$(6 \times 0) + (6 \times 0_2) = 18$ oxygen atoms

$6 \times C = 6$ carbon atoms

On the right:

The reaction produces one molecule of glucose and six molecules of oxygen.

$H_{12} = 12$ hydrogen atoms

$0_6 + (6 \times 0_2) = 18$ oxygen atoms

$C_6 = 6$ carbon atoms

Weird and wonderful reactions

Chemists have discovered all sorts of chemical reactions – some useful and some not so useful. Here are a few examples...

Down on the farm

Dairy farmers often add certain bacteria to cows' milk. The bacteria cause a reaction in the milk that produces a delicious-tasting acid. This is how yoghurt and cheese are made.

Hmm, shall I try propionibacterium or lactobacillus today?

Scorching sunburn

Sunshine contains an invisible energy called ultraviolet light. It causes a reaction in your skin which gives you a tan. But too much leads to sunburn. Sunscreens block the ultraviolet light and prevent the reaction from happening.

Sharp sauce

Soy sauce is made from soy beans and wheat boiled in water. Bacteria in the water 'ferment' (or cause a reaction in) the mixture, breaking it down into alcohols and acids. The acid is what gives soy sauce its sharp taste.

Airy cakes

Baking soda is a sodium compound that produces carbon dioxide when it's heated. It's bubbles of this gas that make a cake rise in the oven.

Catching your breath

Potassium chlorate, lithium chlorate and sodium chlorate all give off oxygen when heated. They are used to provide people in space stations or submarines with oxygen to breathe.

Crippling cramp

Lactic acid is a product of a reaction in your muscles. You use the reaction to get energy when you're doing a lot of exercise. But too much lactic acid can make your muscles ache, and sometimes gives you a cramp.

All kinds of reactions

There are many different ways for substances to react and exchange atoms or ions. Here are just six common types of reaction...

Reaction type 1: trading places

Sometimes, a substance reacts with a compound by kicking out part of that compound. This is called a **displacement reaction**.

For example, zinc metal reacts with hydrochloric acid to displace hydrogen gas. This happens because there's a stronger attraction between zinc and chlorine than between hydrogen and chlorine.

A zinc atom can give an electron to each of two chlorine atoms. The zinc and chlorine become ions and bond with each other. Loose hydrogen atoms are kicked out. They bond in covalent pairs and float away.

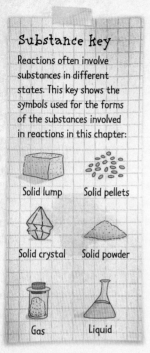

Substance key

Reactions often involve substances in different states. This key shows the symbols used for the forms of the substances involved in reactions in this chapter:

Solid lump   Solid pellets

Solid crystal   Solid powder

Gas   Liquid

How it happens...

Two molecules of hydrochloric acid (hydrogen chloride)...

...meet an atom of zinc.

A-HA! JUST WHAT I NEED TO GET RID OF SOME ELECTRONS.

The zinc atom splits each molecule apart...

I AM ZINC - REACT WITH ME!

And gives one electron to each chlorine atom.

WE DON'T NEED YOU, HYDROGEN!

At the end of the reaction, there's a molecule of zinc chloride, and a molecule of hydrogen.

WELL WE DON'T NEED YOU EITHER!

Chemists say that the zinc has 'displaced' the hydrogen. Here's how it looks as an equation:

$$Zn + 2HCl \rightarrow ZnCl_2 + H_2$$

Reaction type 2: breakdown

If a compound has enough energy, it can sometimes break apart to make new products all by itself. A chemical change has taken place, so this still counts as a chemical reaction. It's called **decomposition**.

For example, when calcium carbonate is heated it breaks apart to form calcium oxide and carbon dioxide gas. Here's the equation:

When a lump of calcium carbonate is heated, it decomposes and releases carbon dioxide gas.

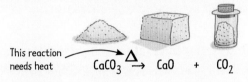

This reaction needs heat

$$CaCO_3 \xrightarrow{\Delta} CaO + CO_2$$

Reaction type 3: back and forth

Sometimes, reactants form new products, only for the products to react together and turn back into the original substances. These are called **reversible reactions**. Because they can keep going back and forth, the reactions never quite finish happening.

For example, if you heat nitrogen dioxide, it splits into nitrogen monoxide and oxygen. This is a decomposition reaction — but it's also reversible. When the products cool down, they react with each other to form nitrogen dioxide again. Heat is the key. If the products stay warm enough, the reverse reaction can't happen.

This equation has an arrow pointing both ways to show that the reaction is reversible:

$$2NO_2 \rightleftharpoons 2NO + O_2$$

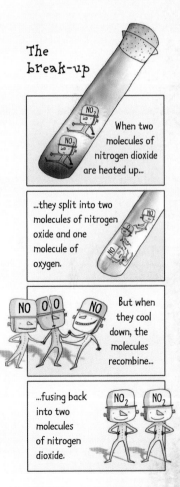

The break-up

When two molecules of nitrogen dioxide are heated up...

...they split into two molecules of nitrogen oxide and one molecule of oxygen.

But when they cool down, the molecules recombine...

...fusing back into two molecules of nitrogen dioxide.

Reaction type 4: two-in-one

Some reactions are made up of two 'half' reactions in which reactants lose and gain electrons.

One reactant loses electrons – this is called **oxidation**. The other reactant gains those electrons – this is called **reduction**. Together, oxidation and reduction make lots of ions – which are then attracted to each other and bond, forming products. The whole process is called a **redox reaction** (short for reduction/oxidation reaction).

One common redox reaction happens between calcium and chlorine. The reaction can be shown as two half equations or one whole equation...

What's in a name?

When oxidation reactions were first discovered, chemists thought they were all about substances gaining oxygen.

Since the discovery of electrons, chemists now know that oxidation is really all about electrons. But the name has stuck.

Oxidation half reaction:
A calcium atom loses two electrons and becomes an ion, written as Ca^{2+}. The calcium is 'oxidized'.

$$Ca \rightarrow Ca^{2+} + 2e^-$$

Reduction half reaction:
A molecule of chlorine gains these two electrons and becomes two ions, written as $2Cl^-$. The chlorine is 'reduced'.

$$Cl_2 + 2e^- \rightarrow 2Cl^-$$

Overall redox reaction:
The calcium ions (Ca^{2+}) bond with the chloride ions (Cl^-), to form the final product: calcium chloride.

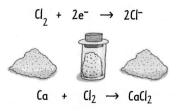

$$Ca + Cl_2 \rightarrow CaCl_2$$

Calcium chloride is an unreactive powder, which is good at absorbing water. It's sometimes used as a food preservative. Chemists use it in labs to protect reactive substances from moisture in the air.

Danger!

This symbol is put on labels to show that a substance is an 'oxidizing agent'.

Most oxidizing agents, such as potassium nitrate, can cause nasty burns. They must be handled with care.

Don't worry – I'll protect you from any mischievous moisture!

54

Blast off!

Burning, or **combustion** as chemists like to
call it, is the most famous redox reaction of all. For
example, in a rocket engine, hydrogen gas burns with
oxygen. A spark activates the reaction between the
two gases, and they keep burning until one runs out.
This reaction gives out a massive amount of heat and
power that pushes the rocket up into space.

Oxidation half reaction:

$$2H_2 \rightarrow 4H^+ + 4e^-$$

Reduction half reaction:

$$O_2 + 4e^- \rightarrow 2O^{2-}$$

**Overall
redox
reaction:**

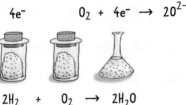

$$2H_2 + O_2 \rightarrow 2H_2O$$

The hydrogen is oxidized and the oxygen is reduced.

**Three-
in-one**

Burning can be
described in
three ways: it's an
exothermic reaction
(it gives out heat), a
combustion reaction
AND a redox reaction.

What a firecracker!

Redox reactions are also the secret behind fireworks.
Fireworks contain a mixture of metal and other
compounds that produce oxygen after they are lit.
The oxygen reacts with the metal, making it burn
with a coloured flame.

Here's the equation for a reaction inside a blue
firework, made using copper chloride:

Oxidation half reaction:

$$4Cl^- \rightarrow 2Cl_2 + 4e^-$$

Reduction half reaction:

$$O_2 + 4e^- \rightarrow 2O^{2-}$$

**Overall
redox
reaction:**

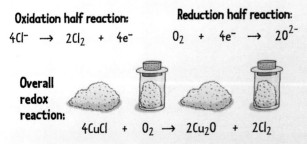

$$4CuCl + O_2 \rightarrow 2Cu_2O + 2Cl_2$$

The chlorine is oxidized and the oxygen is reduced. The copper
starts out bonded to chlorine and ends up bonded to oxygen – so it
has changed – but it hasn't been oxidized or reduced.

Testing, testing

Different metal compounds
burn different colours.
Chemists use the colours as
a simple check to see what
metal a substance contains.
This check is known as a
flame test.

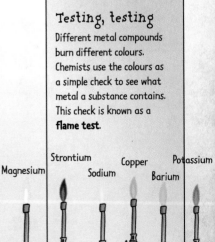

Magnesium   Strontium   Sodium   Copper   Barium   Potassium

Reaction type 5: meet in the middle

Yet another kind of reaction happens when a compound called an **acid** is mixed with a compound called a **base**.

What's an acid?

Acids vary from weak acids — like the sour-tasting citric acid in lemon juice — to strong acids, like the sulphuric acid used in car batteries. Many weak acids are used as flavourings. Strong acids are usually poisonous and are also **corrosive**, meaning they can cause burns.

Chemists define an acid as a substance that makes positive ions of hydrogen (H+) when dissolved in water. How strong the acid is depends on how many of its molecules break up into ions.

What's a base?

A base is the opposite of an acid. In water, it makes negative ions of hydroxide (OH-). Like acids, bases can be strong or weak. Weak bases, such as baking soda, are edible, although they don't taste of much. Strong bases, such as oven cleaner, are as corrosive as strong acids. When a base is dissolved in water, it's called an **alkali**.

A happy medium

When an acid and a base are mixed in the right quantity, they react to form water and a **salt**. Table salt (sodium chloride) is just one kind of salt. Salts aren't acids or bases: they're **neutral**. So this kind of reaction is called a **neutralization reaction**.

This equation shows the neutralization reaction between sodium hydroxide (a base) and hydrochloric acid, which produces table salt and water:

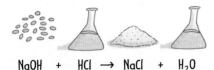

$$NaOH + HCl \rightarrow NaCl + H_2O$$

Water test

Copper sulphate is one of many kinds of salt. When it's dry, it's white, but if it touches even a tiny amount of water, it turns blue. So chemists often use it to test if another substance contains water.

The pH scale

The strength of an acid or a base is measured on a scale called the **pH scale**, which goes from 0 to 14.

A really powerful acid has a pH of 0. The strongest base has a pH of 14. A neutral substance has a pH of 7.

How can you tell them apart?

Luckily for chemists, there's a simple way to tell acids from bases – they use a substance called an **indicator**. One of the simplest indicators is called litmus paper. There are two kinds of litmus paper:

- Blue litmus paper turns red in an acid.
- Red litmus paper turns blue in a base.

Universal indicator can give a more detailed result. It's a liquid that turns red, orange or yellow in acids, pale green in neutral substances, and dark green, blue or purple in bases.

Know your acids from your bases

Acids:	pH
Sulphuric acid	0
Hydrochloric acid	1
Ethanoic acid (in vinegar)	4
Bee sting	5
Citric acid	5
Carbonic acid (in fizzy drinks)	6

Neutral:	
Water	7

Bases:	
Baking soda	8
Soap	8
Wasp sting	9
Magnesium hydroxide (in indigestion tablets)	10
Sodium hydroxide (in drain cleaner)	14

This table shows the colours that universal indicator can turn, depending on the pH of the substance it's mixed with.

Do—it—yourself indicator

You can make your own indicator by following these instructions.

You will need: a red cabbage, a saucepan, some empty glass jars and a variety of household substances to test. You could try: vinegar, mouthwash, orange juice, baking soda, indigestion tablets, peppermint extract — or anything else you like.

1. Chop the red cabbage up into little bits.

2. Boil the cabbage in water for about 10 minutes, until the water turns a pink-purple colour.

3. You don't need the cabbage now. Strain it, and keep the purple liquid. This is your indicator.

4. Allow the indicator to cool, then pour some into a few empty jars.

5. Try adding different substances to the jars, to see which ones make the indicator change colour.

Acids will turn the indicator red.

Bases will turn it blue.

Indicator tip

If a substance is a very weak acid or base you might have to add lots to see a colour change.

You can also make the indicator change colour back and forth by adding an acid first and then lots of a base (or the other way around).

Not quite neutral

When acids and bases mix, they don't always form a neutral product. For example, if you mix a strong base like sodium hydroxide with a weak acid like hydrogen carbonate, it makes a weak base: sodium hydrogen carbonate, more commonly known as baking soda.

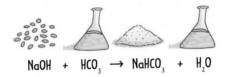

$$NaOH + HCO_3 \rightarrow NaHCO_3 + H_2O$$

In the same way, adding a strong acid to a weak base creates a weak acid. For example, hydrochloric acid and ammonia make ammonium chloride – a weak acid used in shampoo to help prevent split ends in hair.

Soap story

Mixing the right kind of weak acid with the right kind of base makes one very useful product – soap.

Soap contains lots of long chain-like molecules. One end of the chain likes water. That's why a gloopy, soapy mixture forms when you mix soap with water.

The rest of the chain hates water, but loves grease. When you dip greasy hands in soapy water, these ends gather around the grease particles, trapping them. Rinsing with water then allows you to wash away the soap *and* the grease. That's how soap gets things clean.

Bowl of soapy water

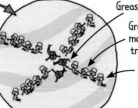

Grease particles

Grease-loving parts of soap molecules gather together, trapping the grease particles.

Water-loving end of soap molecule

what's going on?

When a weak acid reacts with a strong base...

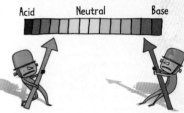

Acid   Neutral   Base

...they don't balance out neutrally. Instead, they make a weak base.

Hands off

Hundreds of years ago, people used to make soap by hand, by mixing animal fat with a base called lye.

But pure lye is so strong that many people burned their hands while making soap. Nowadays people who make soap wear protective clothing.

Reaction type 6: fantastic plastics

Yet another kind of reaction is used in factories that make **plastics**. The reactants are small molecules found in crude oil. Heat, pressure and, sometimes, catalysts make these molecules react to form really long chains, called **polymers**. Chemists call this a **polymerization reaction**.

All plastics are made of polymers. Some polymers exist in nature, too. They're found in things such as wool, cotton and the hairs on your head.

Different plastics have very different properties, making them useful for all sorts of things. Some are hard and strong, others are stretchy and light, and most can be pulled around to make different shapes, from plastic cutlery to toys.

Bulletproof vest

Kevlar® plastic is stitched together to make the vest.

The molecules in Kevlar® are very tightly packed. The structure absorbs and spreads out the impact of a bullet.

Plastic pollution

Many plastics don't break down naturally in rubbish dumps. But some, such as polyester and PET plastic, can easily be recycled.

Plastic fabrics

Plastic is so versatile that it can even be pulled out into thin threads, and woven together to make fabrics that are light, warm and hard-wearing. Lycra® is a plastic used in underwear and sports clothing.

Polyester, another plastic, can be used in pillows, and acrylic plastic is often mixed with wool to weave into warm fleeces.

Reactions: the lowdown

Chemical reactions are happening all the time, everywhere.

A reaction is when the bonds between atoms break and the atoms rearrange themselves into new substances.

1. Two molecules meet.

2. They break apart for a split second.

3. They give, take or share electrons.

4. They form new molecules, called products.

There's always the same amount of matter at the start and end of a reaction.

Bonds are strong – it takes energy to break them, and energy is released when new ones form. The amount of energy needed to start a reaction is called the activation energy.

If more energy is taken in, it's an endothermic reaction.

If more energy is given out, it's an exothermic reaction.

Reactions can be written down as equations using symbols, numbers and arrows.

$$NaOH + HCl \longrightarrow H_2O + NaCl$$
$$\searrow \Delta$$

The triangle means this reaction gives out heat.

Acids and bases are chemical opposites. Their strength is measured in pH units.

There are six common types of reaction:

- displacement
- decomposition
- reversible
- redox
- neutralization
- polymerization

When they react together, they produce neutral salts.

Some reactions involve more than one of these types.

Plastics are made of long chain molecules called polymers.

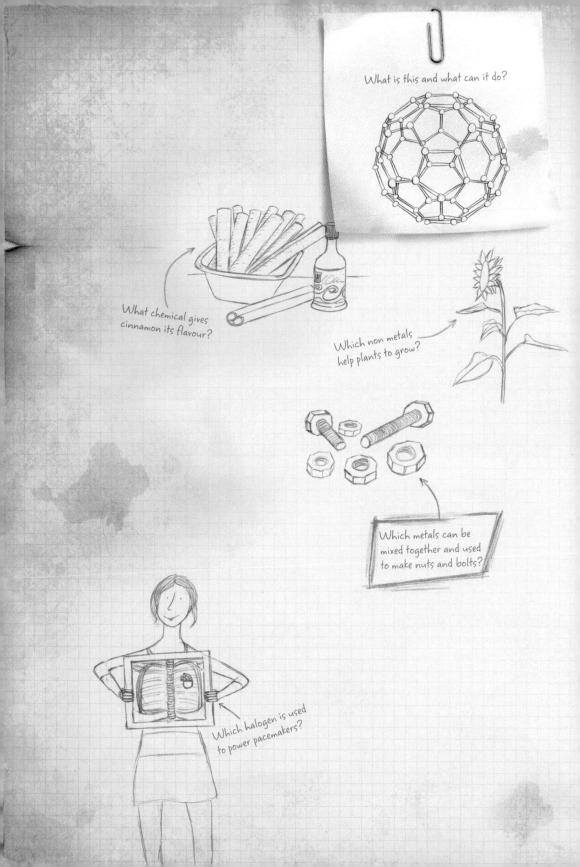

What is this and what can it do?

What chemical gives cinnamon its flavour?

Which non metals help plants to grow?

Which metals can be mixed together and used to make nuts and bolts?

Which halogen is used to power pacemakers?

Part 4:
How is chemistry useful?

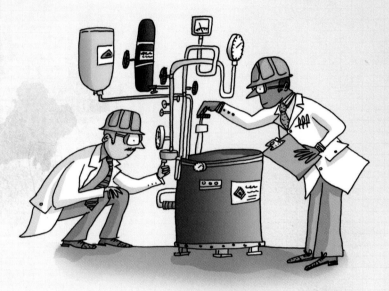

Even before chemists knew anything about molecules, atoms and electron shells, they did experiments to find new ways of using substances – from common carbon and oxygen to rarer stuff such as phosphorus and molybdenum. Along the way, they've worked out how to make all sorts of useful things, some rather unusual and some quite ordinary. In this chapter, you can discover how chemistry plays a role in almost every part of our lives.

Carbon chemistry

Carbon is one of the most useful elements on Earth both as an element and in compounds. Confusingly, pure carbon comes in two main forms which have very different properties: **graphite** and **diamond**.

Graphite is black and crumbly. It's the bit of a pencil that you write with. In graphite, each carbon atom is joined to three others in layers. Each layer can easily slide over the others. That's why the graphite in a pencil rubs off onto paper when you write.

Diamond is the opposite. It's clear and hard – in fact, it's the hardest natural material on Earth. Each carbon atom is bonded to four others in a large, interlocking crystal. This gives diamond its strength. As well as making jewels, it's used in industrial drills.

Bucky balls

'Bucky balls' (short for buckminster fullerenes) are a special form of carbon first discovered in a lab. They look like microscopic footballs, made up of sixty carbon atoms linked together.

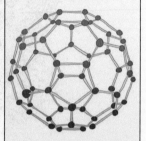

They're really strong and good conductors of electricity. Chemists are exploring ways of using them like incredibly tiny machines, for example to carry molecules of medicine to specific areas of the human body.

Carbon for life

Deep inside you – and every living thing – there are molecules of your very own personal carbon compound, known as **DNA**. It contains hydrogen, nitrogen and some other things, but it's mostly carbon.

The chemicals in your DNA are linked in an order that's unique to you. The order is like a code that tells your body what to do. Your DNA affects everything – from the colour of your eyes to the shape of your nose, and even how good you are at solving puzzles. You inherit half of the code from each of your parents. That's why children and parents share many similar features.

A DNA molecule comes in a shape called a double helix, which looks like this.

Carbon and oxygen

Carbon can bond with another common
element, oxygen, in different ways.

Carbon monoxide (CO) is a colourless,
odourless, and extremely poisonous gas. It's
formed whenever carbon compounds burn
in a limited amount of oxygen, for example in
car engines. Car exhaust fumes contain a lot of
carbon monoxide.

Carbon dioxide (CO_2) is what we breathe out. Plants
absorb it from the air to use in photosynthesis. It's also
used in some kinds of fire extinguisher. Fires need
oxygen to burn, so smothering a flame with carbon
dioxide means that oxygen can't get to it.

Carbon dating

Scientists can use carbon to
date very old remains, such
as this sabretooth tiger skull,
which is over 11,000 years old.

And how does it work? Well,
all living things contain small
amounts of a radioactive type
of carbon called carbon-14 (^{14}C).
After they die, the amount
of ^{14}C gradually decreases.
Scientists can measure how
much is left to work out how
long ago they lived.

Mineral carbon

Many common minerals contain carbon compounds
known as carbonates (CO_3). For example, limestone
rock is mostly calcium carbonate. Lithium carbonate
can be found in anything from glass to glue to pills.

Chemists use carbonates to make carbon dioxide.
If any kind of carbonate is mixed with a strong acid, it
will fizz up and give off carbon dioxide (CO_2) gas.

Testing, testing

Chemists can check if a
reaction produces carbon
dioxide by using a solution of
calcium hydroxide, also known
as limewater.

Limewater is clear. But if it
mixes with carbon dioxide, it
turns cloudy. This is because it
reacts with the gas to make
calcium carbonate – a powder
that doesn't dissolve.

**When calcium carbonate is mixed with
hydrochloric acid, it produces carbon dioxide.**

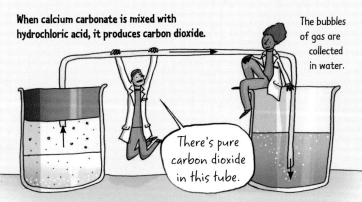

The bubbles
of gas are
collected
in water.

There's pure
carbon dioxide
in this tube.

The reaction also produces water and calcium
chloride (a solid that dissolves in the water).

All about metals

Metals all have similar properties, but some are tougher than others, or better at conducting heat. Here are a few examples of ways people use metals...

Taking the heat

Molybdenum doesn't melt until it reaches an astonishing 2,623°C. It's used on the outside of spacecraft, because it can withstand the intense heat that builds up on re-entry into the Earth's atmosphere.

Hard and soft

Aluminium is the most common metal in the Earth's surface. It's tough but also very light. Thick aluminium makes sturdy frames for cars and trains. Thin sheets of it make crushable drinks cans.

Copper top

Copper conducts electricity well and is often used for electrical wiring. It's also decorative and so is used to make roofs for fancy buildings. It reacts slowly with air to form a protective layer of attractive green copper carbonate.

Body metals

Many reactive metals are found in compounds inside living things. Calcium forms bones and teeth. Potassium makes muscles work. Sodium helps carry signals across nerve cells in the brain.

Do-it-yourself: green copper

You can see for yourself how copper turns green in this simple experiment.

Step 1. Place two copper coins in a cup of vinegar with a little salt for a few minutes until they are shiny.

Step 2. Rinse one of the coins in water. Leave both coins on a windowsill to dry.

You should find that the unrinsed coin starts to turn green after a few hours. But the other coin will stay shiny a while longer.

What's happening? The unrinsed coin reacts with the vinegar and salt solution to form a layer of green copper acetate. The rinsed coin reacts with air to form a layer of green copper oxide (this reaction normally takes longer).

Alloy, alloy, alloy!

Different metals can be combined to make metal-based mixtures known as **alloys**. Alloys are useful because they combine properties of all the elements in them.

The earliest man-made alloy was so useful that it spread around the world and gave its name to a whole period of history – the Bronze Age. Bronze is made by melting and mixing together copper and tin. It's strong (like copper) and resists corrosion (like tin).

Bronze is often used to make statues.

Inside bronze, atoms of copper and tin jumble together. Most bronze contains a lot more copper than tin.

Brass tacks

Brass is an alloy of copper and zinc. It's used to make all sorts of bits and pieces, such as nuts, bolts and tacks because it's tough.

Soldering on

Solder is made of tin and silver or lead. It melts at low temperatures, and is useful for sealing metal joints and building electronic circuits.

The secret of steel

Special alloys can also be made by mixing metals with non metals. The most famous is steel, an alloy of iron and carbon. A small amount of carbon keeps the iron atoms in a rigid structure, making steel super tough.

Steel is harder to make than bronze, because iron needs very high temperatures to melt. But it's easier to find iron because there's lots of it in the ground. Today steel is used to make things that need to be really strong, such as the frames of skyscrapers. Steel can also be mixed with chromium to stop it from rusting. This 'stainless' steel is used to make cutlery.

The perfect sword

Some of the first steel-makers were swordsmiths in Japan. They melted and re-forged their blades many times over. This made the carbon and iron atoms spread out more evenly, making the blades extra tough.

67

Wrestling with reactions

Some metals are more willing to react than others. All metals can be listed in order of their willingness to react – this is called the **reactivity series**.

One way of picturing the series is to imagine all the metals are taking part in a wrestling competition. The metals that win the most fights are the most reactive.

For example, when zinc chloride is mixed with magnesium, zinc and magnesium 'compete' to form a bond with chlorine. Magnesium is more reactive than zinc, so it 'wins' the competition, and bonds with chlorine to form magnesium chloride.

Here's how some of the most useful metals stack up against each other in the reactivity series:

Metal reactions

All metals share some chemical properties as well as physical ones. These three reactions will produce the same kind of product with any metal.

Any metal + oxygen
→ a metal oxide

Any metal + a strong acid
→ a salt + hydrogen

Any metal + superhot steam
→ a metal oxide + hydrogen

Just face it, I'm more reactive than you!

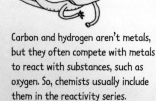

I may not be a metal, but I'll take you all on!

Carbon and hydrogen aren't metals, but they often compete with metals to react with substances, such as oxygen. So, chemists usually include them in the reactivity series.

Most reactive

Potassium (K)
Sodium (Na)
Calcium (Ca)
Magnesium (Mg)
Aluminium (Al)
Carbon (C)
Zinc (Zn)
Iron (Fe)
Tin (Sn)
Lead (Pb)
Hydrogen (H)
Copper (Cu)
Silver (Ag)
Gold (Au)
Platinum (Pt)

Least reactive

You'll never beat me!

I always lose.

Using gases

Hydrogen and helium are the two most common elements in the Universe. They're both colourless and odourless gases.

If you've ever seen party balloons that float up to the ceiling, they were full of helium. Helium is less dense than air, so a helium balloon will rise until it hits something. Outside, it will drift up until the air pressure gets so weak that the pressure of the helium pushing outwards inside the balloon makes it burst.

Hydrogen is also less dense than air. Some of the first 'airships' were filled with a mixture of air and hydrogen, to make them rise. But, because hydrogen burns very easily, many accidents happened. Modern airships use helium instead, because it's much safer, even though it's harder to get than hydrogen.

Oxygen is the third most common element in the Universe. Pure oxygen is one of the gases found in air. People need to breathe it to survive. It's also needed for things to combust, or burn.

Oxygen is very reactive and forms many compounds called oxides. The most common of these is water. Another is hydrogen peroxide (H_2O_2), a pale blue liquid also known as bleach. It has lots of uses – killing bacteria, making hair dyes, and even as a fuel for prototype space rockets.

DIY voicechanger

Step 1. Open the end of a helium balloon and carefully suck in a mouthful of gas.

Step 2. Say something...

Eeeeeee!

...You should find that your voice sounds really squeaky.

What's going on?
Because helium is lighter than air, it makes the vocal cords in your throat vibrate faster. This makes your voice sound high and squeaky.

Burning question

For a long time, even the cleverest scientists weren't sure what made things burn.

In the 1770s, three chemists – Frenchman Antoine Lavoisier, Englishman Joseph Priestley and German Carl Scheele, all found the answer independently...

It's oxygen!

What about non metals?

There aren't very many non metals, but they're found in some of the most useful substances on Earth.

Explosive nitrogen

TNT is a well-known explosive. It's named after the nitrogen compound it contains: tri-nitro-toluene. Chemist Joseph Wilbrand invented TNT as a yellow dye in 1863. Its explosive properties weren't discovered until decades later.

No flies on phosphorus

The compound phosphorus trihydride is a poisonous gas. It's used to kill pests which eat grain. Farmers only use a mild form of it, so the grain isn't poisoned as well.

Fertilizers

Nitrogen and phosphorus are both major ingredients in fertilizers. They help farmers to grow more plants in places with poor soil.

Using the halogens

The halogens are very reactive non metals. Some of them are quite dangerous, but chemists have still found uses for them.

Boring bromine

In the past, doctors used bromine compounds, called bromides, to help people to sleep. For many years, the word 'bromide' just meant anything really boring.

Medical iodine

When solid iodine is dissolved in alcohol, it's a strong antiseptic which can be used to treat wounds.

Lithium iodide is used in the batteries of pacemakers. These are tiny machines that help steady a person's heartbeat.

Choking on chlorine

Chlorine is used in carefully controlled amounts to disinfect swimming pools and drinking water.

Pure chlorine gas is so poisonous, it was used as a weapon in the First World War. Soldiers had to protect themselves from it by wearing gas masks.

Pacemakers can be seen by an X-ray.

What a stink!

Chemistry labs can be full of strange and terrible smells. One of the smelliest chemicals is sulphur, but it's not the only culprit...

Smelly food

Sulphur is found in rotten eggs, which have a really unpleasant smell. It's also what gives garlic its strong taste, in a compound called allicin.

Smelling salts

When a person faints, one way to revive them can be to release a strong smell. Smelling salts react with air to release a tiny amount of ammonia gas, which can sometimes do the trick.

Skunk spray

Skunks spray a horrible smell that sends any attackers running. It's full of sulphur compounds called thiols. The smell is so strong it can spread for over a mile. The spray can even cause temporary blindness if aimed at the eyes.

Dead smelly

Some nitrogen compounds have very strong smells, with names that match! Putrescine and cadaverine are the compounds that make rotting (or 'putrescent') things and dead bodies (or 'cadavers') smell awful.

Fume cupboard

Some chemical reactions create very smelly and even dangerous gases. Chemists do these reactions inside a fume cupboard. A fan in the top of the cupboard whisks the gases safely away.

Butyric acid

One common smell is very hard to forget. Butyric acid wafts up from parmesan cheese, rancid butter, vomit and even from people who don't wash.

Chemical curiosities

Every day, clever chemists around the world are unlocking the chemistry of substances and finding out how things work. All sorts of things happen because of chemistry – some that you might never have thought of...

Why do I like chocolate?

Chocolate contains two delightful compounds – tryptophan and theobromine – which react with the body to produce hormones that make people feel happy and relaxed.

Detective work

It's not always easy to tell dried blood from dried ketchup or other red substances. Detectives spray a compound called luminol onto suspicious red stains. If there's any blood, the luminol will glow blue.

Flavourings

Cinnamaldehyde is the chemical that gives natural cinnamon its flavour. The same chemical can be made in labs and factories, and used as an artifical flavouring.

Lawn lovers

Hexenal is the substance that gives freshly cut grass its particular smell. Some insects also produce it as a scent to attract their mates.

Preserving specimens

Formaldehyde is a strong-smelling liquid used to preserve animal specimens and human organs. It soaks into them and stops them from decaying.

A brain preserved in formaldehyde

Mad hatters

In the 19th century, mercury was used to make hats shiny. But inhaling the fumes made some hat-makers rant, rave and shake. This is where the phrase 'as mad as a hatter' comes from.

How to tell what's what

Identifying different elements and compounds can be a tricky business. Big labs often have an incredibly useful machine called a mass spectrometer to do that.

What happens inside a mass spectrometer?

1. Inside the machine, a dissolved sample is boiled into a gas and then turned into ions.

2. The ions are exposed to electricity and a powerful magnet.

3. This makes them fly through a chamber at different speeds and angles, depending on their mass and electric charge.

Finally, a computer produces a graph showing the amounts and masses of the different ions in the sample.

Walk-in testing

Some airports have giant pods that passengers step into. A mass spectrometer is attached to the pod.

The pod quickly sucks in particles on the passengers' clothes and the mass spectrometer checks these particles for any traces of illegal drugs or explosives.

Micro-investigations

One way to find out about a substance is to get a really good look at it. Here are two methods that can help chemists do this...

X-tra special

The way X-rays shine through or bounce off the surface of crystals gives clues about how the molecules hold together.

Rosalind Franklin used a technique called X-ray crystallography on crystals of DNA. Her work was vital to understanding its structure.

Franklin's X-ray image

Copper oxide crystals seen by SEM

Mighty microscopes

A scanning electron microscope (SEM) can see tiny details that a normal microscope cannot. It fires a stream of electrons at the surface of a substance, and records where other electrons are knocked off it. The machine uses this data to create a computer image of the surface.

Careful! It might be dangerous.

But what is it?

Is there a simple way to find out what a substance is?

In a high-tech lab, professional chemists would use a mass spectrometer to identify a mysterious substance. But you don't always need big machines to identify substances. There are simple tests that you can try out in a school lab. This two-stage chemical sorter will help you to work out what kind of substance a mystery solid is.

Sorter stage one

First, you need to make sure you've got a pure element or compound, and not a mixture. You could try a few separation techniques (see pages 20-23). Here are some of the questions you can ask and tests you can do to help you identify a substance. It's not always possible to get a precise answer.

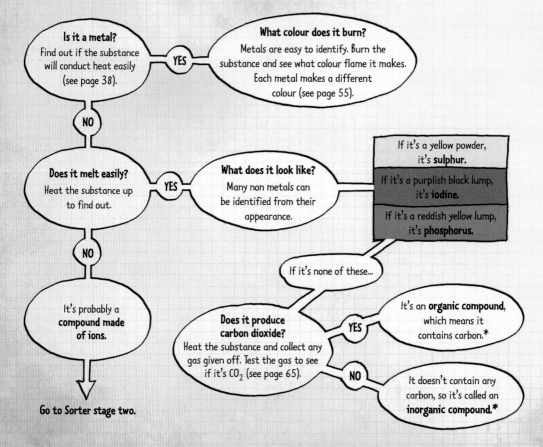

Is it a metal?
Find out if the substance will conduct heat easily (see page 38).

YES

What colour does it burn?
Metals are easy to identify. Burn the substance and see what colour flame it makes. Each metal makes a different colour (see page 55).

NO

Does it melt easily?
Heat the substance up to find out.

YES

What does it look like?
Many non metals can be identified from their appearance.

If it's a yellow powder, it's **sulphur**.

If it's a purplish black lump, it's **iodine**.

If it's a reddish yellow lump, it's **phosphorus**.

NO

It's probably a **compound made of ions.**

If it's none of these...

Does it produce carbon dioxide?
Heat the substance and collect any gas given off. Test the gas to see if it's CO_2 (see page 65).

YES

It's an **organic compound**, which means it contains carbon.*

NO

It doesn't contain any carbon, so it's called an **inorganic compound.***

Go to Sorter stage two.

Sorter stage two

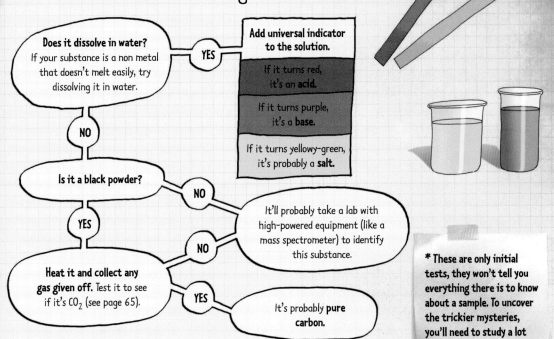

Does it dissolve in water?
If your substance is a non metal that doesn't melt easily, try dissolving it in water.

YES

Add universal indicator to the solution.

If it turns red, it's an **acid.**

If it turns purple, it's a **base.**

If it turns yellowy-green, it's probably a **salt.**

NO

Is it a black powder?

NO

YES

NO

It'll probably take a lab with high-powered equipment (like a mass spectrometer) to identify this substance.

Heat it and collect any gas given off. Test it to see if it's CO$_2$ (see page 65).

YES

It's probably **pure carbon.**

* These are only initial tests, they won't tell you everything there is to know about a sample. To uncover the trickier mysteries, you'll need to study a lot more chemistry!

Can I identify colourless gases?

When chemists do reactions, they usually have an idea of what products will form. Many reactions produce oxygen or hydrogen as by-products. So, to check a reaction has worked, chemists can test for these gases.
Here are two tests you can try in a school lab:

POP!

For both tests:
1. Collect the gas in a test tube. Put a stopper on it.

2. Light a piece of wood often called a splint.

To test for hydrogen:
Place the lit splint into the test tube. If it's hydrogen, the splint will go pop and the flame will go out.

To test for oxygen:
Blow out the flame, then stick the smouldering splint into the test tube. If it's oxygen, the splint will re-light.

Part 5:
Our chemical Universe

The Universe and all the stars and planets in it – including our own planet, the Earth – were formed by chemical processes billions of years ago. Ever since then, chemistry has been making changes all day, every day, to the land, sea and sky. Chemistry is also involved in the life and death of all living things, including human beings. Read on to find out how elements are formed, what rocks and air are made of, and what chemicals your body needs to survive.

Where did the elements come from?

Most scientists think that the Universe exploded into existence about $14\frac{1}{2}$ billion years ago. At first, there was only one element – hydrogen. There were billions and billions and billions of hydrogen atoms, all squashed up into baby stars.

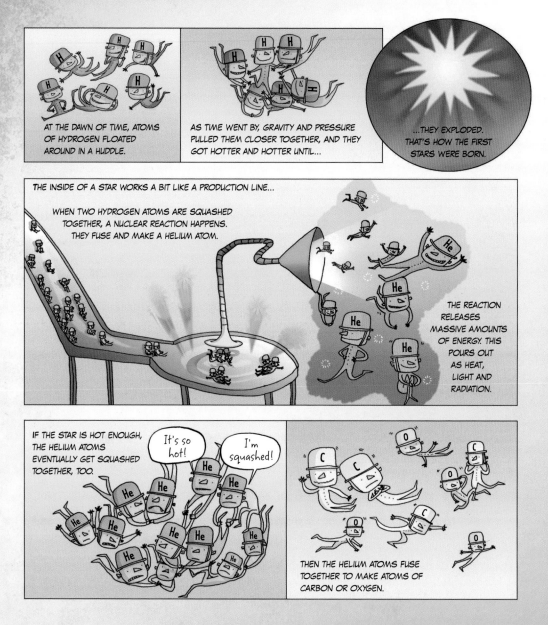

AT THE DAWN OF TIME, ATOMS OF HYDROGEN FLOATED AROUND IN A HUDDLE.

AS TIME WENT BY, GRAVITY AND PRESSURE PULLED THEM CLOSER TOGETHER, AND THEY GOT HOTTER AND HOTTER UNTIL...

...THEY EXPLODED. THAT'S HOW THE FIRST STARS WERE BORN.

THE INSIDE OF A STAR WORKS A BIT LIKE A PRODUCTION LINE...

WHEN TWO HYDROGEN ATOMS ARE SQUASHED TOGETHER, A NUCLEAR REACTION HAPPENS. THEY FUSE AND MAKE A HELIUM ATOM.

THE REACTION RELEASES MASSIVE AMOUNTS OF ENERGY. THIS POURS OUT AS HEAT, LIGHT AND RADIATION.

IF THE STAR IS HOT ENOUGH, THE HELIUM ATOMS EVENTUALLY GET SQUASHED TOGETHER, TOO.

It's so hot!

I'm squashed!

THEN THE HELIUM ATOMS FUSE TOGETHER TO MAKE ATOMS OF CARBON OR OXYGEN.

AS NEW, HEAVIER ELEMENTS ARE MADE, THE STAR BECOMES DENSER...

...AND MUCH, MUCH HOTTER.

INSIDE A REALLY BIG, HOT, DENSE STAR, EVEN HEAVIER ELEMENTS CAN BE MADE...

...AND MORE HEAT, LIGHT AND RADIATION ARE GIVEN OUT.

EVENTUALLY, THE STAR BECOMES SO SMALL AND HOT THAT IT EXPLODES - THIS EXPLOSION IS CALLED A SUPERNOVA.

A SUPERNOVA IS SO POWERFUL THAT THE STAR DIES, AND ALL THE ATOMS IN IT GO FLYING OUT ACROSS THE UNIVERSE.

GRADUALLY SOME OF THESE ATOMS CLUSTER TOGETHER INSIDE NEW STARS, WHICH IN TURN FORM MASSIVE GALAXIES

SOME STARS HAVE A SOLAR SYSTEM OF PLANETS. THE PLANETS ARE MADE OUT OF A MIXTURE OF ELEMENTS FROM LONG DEAD STARS.

THE SUN IN OUR SOLAR SYSTEM IS A ONLY A MEDIUM-SIZED STAR...

...INSIDE IT, HYDROGEN IS TURNED INTO HELIUM. BUT IT'S NOT HOT ENOUGH TO MAKE HEAVIER ELEMENTS.

Rocks are chemicals too

The surface of the Earth is made of rock – both on land and under the sea. Rocks might look like lumps that never do anything. But, like everything else, they're actually taking part in chemical reactions.

Cave chemistry

Inside limestone caves, extraordinary natural sculptures are built very slowly.

Step 1. When it rains, water trickles into the cave, dissolving tiny bits of limestone.

Step 2. The water drips down from the roof and lands on the floor of the cave.

Step 3. The water evaporates and leaves little bits of limestone behind.

Over thousands of years, these tiny deposits build up to create rock formations.

Stalagmites rise up from the cave floor; stalactites hang down from the ceiling.

Breaking mountains

Most mountains have tiny cracks in their rock faces. Rainwater flows into these cracks, and often freezes into ice. Ice takes up more space than water, forcing the crack to widen.

After many thousands of years of rain and ice, the crack gets so wide that part of the mountain simply falls off.

There are three main types of rock...

1. Igneous

The inside of the Earth contains molten (melted) rock, called **magma**. This gradually cools to form **igneous** rocks, such as granite or pumice.

Mt. Rushmore, USA is made of granite, an igneous rock.

2. Sedimentary

Sedimentary rocks are formed when tiny bits of rocks, bones and shells get squashed together, often underwater, making one gigantic new rock, such as chalk or sandstone.

The white horse of Kilburn, UK, is carved from sandstone and covered in a layer of chalk.

3. Metamorphic

Metamorphic rocks form when other rocks are heated and squashed underground. A chemical reaction creates a new type of hard, shiny rock, such as marble or slate.

A Roman tomb sculpted out of metamorphic marble.

The rock cycle

The rocks on Earth are all constantly changing, very, very slowly. So if you could travel far into the future, you'd see quite a different landscape. Mountains would have moved and changed shape, and rocks of one kind would have changed into another.

Wind and rain **erode** (wear away) surface rocks, grinding large rocks into tiny pieces of sediment. Over millions of years, this sediment builds up and gets squashed, creating new sedimentary rocks. Deep underground, intense pressures and high temperatures convert igneous and sedimentary rocks into new, metamorphic types. Eventually, these rocks can get squished down into the Earth's superhot interior, where they melt back into magma. This is called the **rock cycle**.

Moving Earth

Deep underground it's hot enough to melt rocks into a liquid. This molten rock sits in a layer called the **mantle**, below the Earth's surface.

On top of the mantle, the surface – or **crust** – is divided into sections called plates. These plates are constantly moving – but normally very, very slowly.

The rock cycle is happening around us all the time. But each stage of the cycle takes thousands of years.

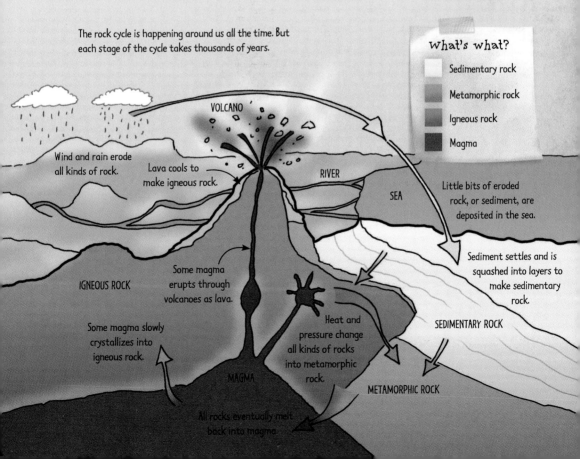

what's what?

- Sedimentary rock
- Metamorphic rock
- Igneous rock
- Magma

VOLCANO

Wind and rain erode all kinds of rock.

Lava cools to make igneous rock.

RIVER

SEA

Little bits of eroded rock, or sediment, are deposited in the sea.

Sediment settles and is squashed into layers to make sedimentary rock.

IGNEOUS ROCK

Some magma erupts through volcanoes as lava.

Some magma slowly crystallizes into igneous rock.

Heat and pressure change all kinds of rocks into metamorphic rock.

SEDIMENTARY ROCK

MAGMA

METAMORPHIC ROCK

All rocks eventually melt back into magma.

What's up in the air?

The Earth comes equipped with its own air protection system – called the **atmosphere**. The atmosphere is a mixture of gases that blankets the Earth and it's responsible for the weather, and the air you breathe.

High up in the Earth's atmosphere, a layer of gas called ozone (O_3) protects the Earth from some harmful rays from the Sun. Below this layer, gases such as carbon dioxide keep the Earth warm by trapping heat.

Since the invention of power stations, factories and cars, people have been releasing a lot of harmful gases into the atmosphere. These pollute the air, making it harder to breathe. Some create acid rain, which poisons plants and corrodes buildings. And some of these gases react with ozone, making holes in the ozone layer.

Lightning gas

When a bolt of lightning strikes, it leaves behind a strange smell. This is the smell of ozone gas. At ground level too much ozone is an air pollutant and can cause breathing problems.

What's up there?

The atmosphere is made up of four main layers...

Thermosphere – this is full of ions that block some harmful rays from the Sun.

Mesosphere – it's very cold here.

The **ozone layer** is in the upper stratosphere.

Stratosphere – this is where planes fly.

Troposphere – this is where weather happens.

The greenhouse effect

Carbon dioxide is sometimes described as a greenhouse gas, because it acts like an insulating blanket around the planet, stopping heat from escaping. Without any greenhouse gases, the Earth would be too cold for people to survive. But many scientists worry that we are pumping too much carbon dioxide into the air and over-heating the Earth. This process is known as the **greenhouse effect**.

Fossil fuels, such as oil and coal, contain many carbon compounds. As these are burned, they react with oxygen to produce lots of carbon dioxide. Other greenhouse gases include methane and the gases in aerosol sprays. Scientists are working to find ways to generate energy without releasing harmful gases.

Living chemistry

Plants and animals are brimming with chemical secrets. Some of them are deadly poisons, but many others are sources of wonderful medicines.

A puffer fish shows its deadly spikes.

Frog of doom

Poison-dart frogs from South America excrete a poison called batrachotoxin through their skin. The poison causes heart failure in small animals that attack the frog. Some rainforest peoples extract the poison to use on the tips of their hunting darts.

Fish of doom

Pufferfish have a deadly poison called tetrodotoxin in their skin, spikes and organs. This kills any predator that tries to bite or squash them.

Death to Socrates!

In Ancient Greece, the philosopher Socrates was sentenced to death for teaching dangerous ideas. He was poisoned with the plant hemlock, which contains a deadly chemical called coniine.

Natural medicines

In the past, people all over the world have turned to plants to help fight pain or cure diseases. Nowadays, chemists can identify the active ingredients of many plants and copy them in labs to make medicines.

The Qincocha Indians chewed the bark from willow trees to cure fever. It contains acetylsalicylic acid, which is now used to make aspirin. It blocks pain and reduces fevers.

Nearly 2,500 years ago, the Sumerians used mint leaves to cure stomach aches. The leaves contain a compound called menthol, which has soothing properties.

The Romans used feverfew plants to treat headaches. The active ingredient is a compound called parthenolide, which eases aches and swelling.

How does your body work?

Your body depends on chemistry to keep it going. It uses thousands of compounds to stay alive and well.

People and most other animals have an iron-based compound called hemoglobin in their blood. It helps transport oxygen from the lungs to the rest of the body. This form of iron is the reason your blood is red. Some sea creatures, such as horseshoe crabs, have another compound called hemocyanin — it's made of copper instead of iron, which makes their blood blue.

Blood test

Blue blood extracted from horseshoe crabs reacts with bacteria. Doctors can use it to test that new medicines are bacteria-free.

A horseshoe crab

You are what you eat

Most food contains carbon, hydrogen and oxygen, which your body uses for energy.

You also need to eat tiny amounts of some metals and other elements. Your body uses these for things like growing, repairing damage and fighting disease.

Cabbage leaves are full of phosphorus, which strengthens the immune system.

Blue cheese has lots of sodium, for a healthy brain and nerves.

Spinach contains iron, for healthy blood.

Beef contains potassium and phosphorous, for healthy nerves and bones.

Shellfish contain selenium, which helps to control chemical signals in the body.

A lifetime of chemistry

Some chemical reactions happen inside your body every minute of every day. But there are some important reactions that only happen at certain stages of life...

Starting out

A new mother has lots of the hormone oxytocin in her system. It helps her bond with her baby.

Virus killer

When people catch a virus, such as chicken pox, the body activates a protein named interferon. Interferon generates chemicals called antibodies that fight off the virus. It also stops people getting ill from the same virus twice.

Sleeping late

Melatonin is a hormone which tells your body to sleep. Usually the brain releases it in the evening. But many teenagers stay up late because their melatonin is released later at night. It keeps them in bed for longer in the morning, too.

Loved up

Falling in love sends two hormones called dopamine and serotonin racing around the body and brain. They make people feel warm, cuddly emotions.

Pain and pleasure

When a person does a lot of exercise, the brain releases hormones called endorphins. They pump around the body, blocking pain and making the person feel good.

Death swell

After a person dies, the bacteria in the body start to break it down. This produces gases underneath the skin that make the body bulge and turn green.

Turning grey

Hair colour comes from a compound called melanin. As some people get older, their hair produces less melanin. Eventually, there's no colour left and their hair turns white.

What is an experiment?

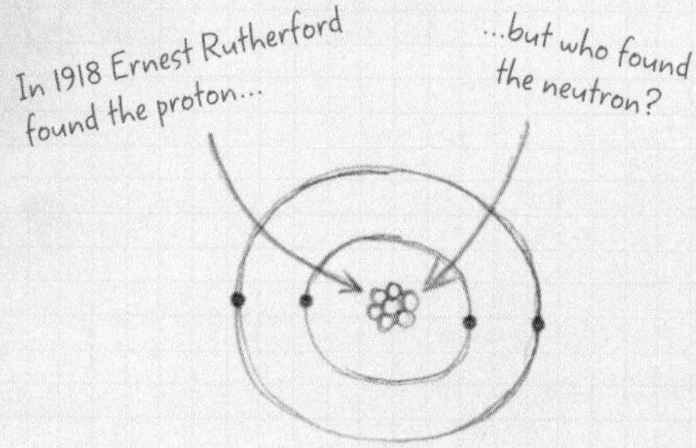
In 1918 Ernest Rutherford found the proton...
...but who found the neutron?

What's this contraption?

Why do good experiments involve at least two observations?
A
B

When did humans figure out how to create fire?

Part 6:
More about chemistry

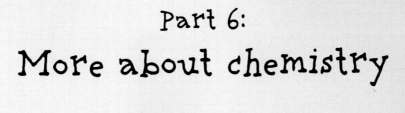

In this section you can find out more about how
science works, and how to do your own
chemistry experiments. You can also find out
about some of the most important advances in
chemistry since people first rubbed sticks
together to create fire.

Chemistry through the ages

People have been studying substances for thousands of years. In about 750, Arab scholars named this work *al quemia*, meaning 'the chemistry'. This term was translated into English as 'alchemy'. This early science gradually evolved into what we know today as 'chemistry'...

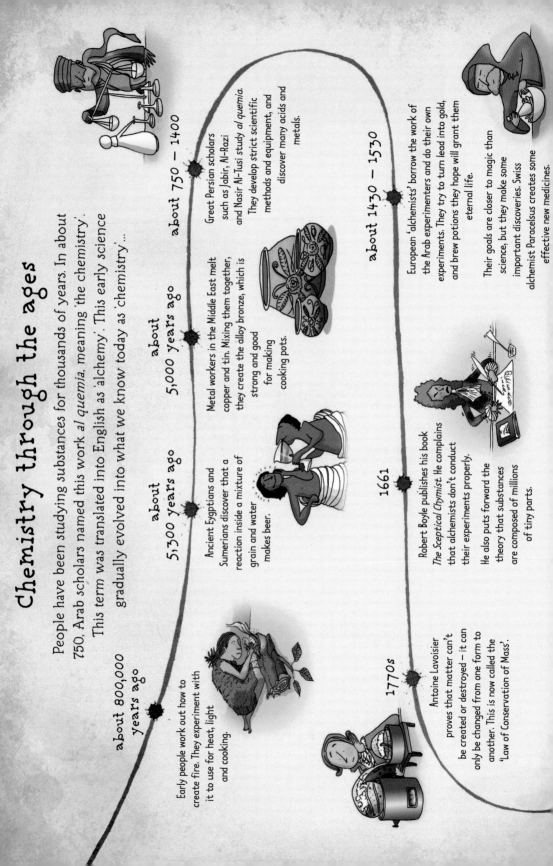

about 800,000 years ago

Early people work out how to create fire. They experiment with it to use for heat, light and cooking.

about 5,300 years ago

Ancient Egyptians and Sumerians discover that a reaction inside a mixture of grain and water makes beer.

about 5,000 years ago

Metal workers in the Middle East melt copper and tin. Mixing them together, they create the alloy bronze, which is strong and good for making cooking pots.

about 750 – 1400

Great Persian scholars such as Jabir, Al-Razi and Nasir Al-Tusi study *al quemia*. They develop strict scientific methods and equipment, and discover many acids and metals.

about 1430 – 1530

European 'alchemists' borrow the work of the Arab experimenters and do their own experiments. They try to turn lead into gold, and brew potions they hope will grant them eternal life.

Their goals are closer to magic than science, but they make some important discoveries. Swiss alchemist Paracelsus creates some effective new medicines.

1661

Robert Boyle publishes his book *The Sceptical Chymist*. He complains that alchemists don't conduct their experiments properly.

He also puts forward the theory that substances are composed of millions of tiny parts.

1770s

Antoine Lavoisier proves that matter can't be created or destroyed – it can only be changed from one form to another. This is now called the 'Law of Conservation of Mass'.

1800

Alessandro Volta experiments with metals and salts, and constructs his 'Voltaic pile' – the first battery.

1810s

Humphry Davy discovers and names new elements such as sodium, potassium, calcium, magnesium and chlorine.

1800s–30s

John Dalton develops an accurate theory of atoms from his studies of gases and evaporation.

1848

Lord Kelvin gives his name to a new temperature scale. 0 Kelvin, or 'absolute zero', is a temperature so cold that it would make atoms stop moving.

1869

Dmitri Mendeleev arranges all known elements into a Periodic Table. He deliberately leaves room for undiscovered elements to fit into the grid.

1897

J.J. Thompson studies beams of light called cathode rays. He finds tiny, negatively charged particles that we now know as electrons.

1898

Marie and Pierre Curie isolate two new radioactive elements, radium and polonium, from coal dust.

1915–1923

George Washington Carver helps American farmers to grow healthy, cheap crops by replacing soil nutients with fertilizers. He also finds hundreds of uses for compounds he extracts from peanuts.

1918

Ernest Rutherford finds the proton...

1932

...and James Chadwick finds the neutron.

1985

Buckminster fullerenes are discovered. This begins a new branch of science, called nanotechnology, as scientists investigate how these 'bucky balls' can be used to make super-tiny machines.

2001

A new anti-cancer drug called Glivec® is developed by teams of chemists. Many other new life-saving drugs are being researched every day.

What is science?

Science comes from the Latin word, *scientia*, meaning 'knowledge'. It is the study of how things work, and is often divided into three areas:

Chemistry is about the substances that make up the world.

Biology is the study of life.

Physics is the study of the laws that rule our Universe.

How does chemistry work?

Chemists (and all other kinds of scientists too) come up with ideas that explain something about the world. They base those ideas on things they've seen, or that other chemists have written about.

Then they have to see if their ideas are right. To be a real scientist, it isn't enough to say that what you *think* is true, or that you believe it, or that it's common sense. You have to *prove* it's right (or at least, not wrong), by doing experiments that back it up. When an idea can be tested through experiments, it's called a **hypothesis** (unlike the many ideas people have which can't be tested scientifically).

Top scientists write about their experiments in journals, so other scientists around the world can try them too. If other experts agree there is enough evidence, the hypothesis becomes a **theory** – that means, it's the accepted, tested and most likely explanation of why something is the way it is.

How do experiments work?

An experiment must be a fair test of an idea.

1. Hypothesis
This is where you explain what your idea is. It also usually includes predictions of what you expect the results of the experiment to be.

2. Method
This describes how you're going to do the experiment. It includes a **control**, which is the 'normal' situation; and the experiment, which is like the control but with one key difference. That way, if the results vary, you know it must be because of that one thing.

3. Results
These record the outcome of the experiment (including the control).

4. Conclusion
This is where you interpret the results. Did they support the hypothesis? Have you changed or rejected your hypothesis after seeing the results?

Here's an example of a simple scientific experiment...

1. Hypothesis
'Adding salt to ice makes it melt faster.'

2. Method
Place two ice cubes in separate glasses. Sprinkle a teaspoon of salt on ice cube B, but none on ice cube A. Time how long the ice cubes take to melt. Do they melt at the same speed, or does one melt faster than the other?

3. Results
Ice cube B melts faster than ice cube A (the control).

4. Conclusion
The only difference between the ice cubes was that one was exposed to salt and one wasn't. So ice cube B must have melted faster because of the added salt. This result supports the hypothesis.

However, there might be reasons why this experiment wouldn't work. For example, ice cube B might be slightly warmer or smaller than the control, ice cube A. If it's already warmer or smaller, this ice cube might take less time to melt. It's really important to make sure that the salt is the *only* difference between the ice cubes.

Are scientists ever wrong?

Yes, scientists get things wrong all the time. They may misinterpret experiments, get bad results, or not be able to test ideas until the right technology is invented.

But what every good scientist wants most of all is to discover how things really work – even if that means admitting to mistakes along the way. So, if their ideas are proved wrong, they're always prepared to change what they think, and move on.

'The one who seeks truth ... submits to argument and demonstration'

This was the philosophy of one of the first people to use fair, rigorous experiments.

Ibn al-Haytham, an 11th-century scholar, based his theories about light and vision on his own observations, rather than what people usually assumed was true.

He argued that scholars shouldn't trust anyone's ideas without carefully considering the evidence for themselves.

Glossary

Words in *italics* have their own separate entries.

acid A *substance* that forms positive *ions* of hydrogen (H^+) when *dissolved* in water.

activation energy The minimum amount of energy *substances* need to *react* together.

alkali A *base dissolved* in water.

alloy A *mixture* formed from two or more *metals*, or from a *metal* and a *non metal*.

alpha particle A form of *radiation* made up of two *protons* and two *neutrons*.

atom The smallest building block of an *element*.

atomic number The number of *protons* in the *nucleus* of an *atom* of a certain *element*.

base A *substance* that forms negative *ions* of hydroxide (OH^-) when *dissolved* in water.

boiling point The *temperature* at which a *substance* changes *state* from a liquid to a gas.

bond A link between *atoms* or *ions* in a *molecule*.

by-product Another *reaction product* that is not the main or useful product.

catalyst A chemical that speeds up the *rate of reaction*, but is not a *reactant*.

chemical equation A way of writing down the *reactants*, *products* and conditions of a *reaction*.

chemical reaction The breaking and forming of *bonds* that changes *reactants* into *products*.

chemical symbol One or two letters that stand for an *element's* name, for example He for helium.

combustion The burning of a *substance* in air.

compound A *substance* made up of two or more different *elements* that have *bonded* together.

condensing When a gas changes into a liquid.

conducting The carrying of heat or an electric charge.

corrode To wear away or rust a *metal*.

covalent bond A *bond* that involves the sharing of *electrons* between *atoms*.

crystal A regular, repeating arrangement of *atoms*, *molecules* or *ions* inside a solid.

decomposition reaction A *reaction* in which a *compound* breaks down into smaller parts.

displacement reaction A *reaction* in which one *element* replaces another in a *compound*.

dissolve To mix a *substance* into a liquid, forming a *solution*.

distillation A purification process that isolates different *substances* due to their different *boiling points*.

electrolysis A process where a liquid *compound* is split apart by passing an electric current through it.

electron A tiny, negatively charged particle that orbits an *atom's nucleus*.

element The simplest type of *substance*, made up of only one sort of *atom*.

endothermic reaction A *reaction* that takes in a lot of heat and gives out only a little.

erode To wear away an object by the action of wind, rain or *chemical reactions*.

evaporating When a liquid changes into a gas.

exothermic reaction A *reaction* that takes in only a little heat and gives out a lot.

freezing point The *temperature* at which a *substance* changes *state* from a liquid to a solid.

greenhouse effect An increase in the average temperature on Earth, caused by a build up of gases in the atmosphere that don't allow heat to escape.

groups The columns of the *Periodic Table* numbered I-VIII. *Elements* in the same group often have very similar *properties*.

indicator A *substance* that turns a specific colour when mixed with an *acid* or a *base*.

inhibitor A *substance* that decreases the *rate of reaction*.

ion An *atom* that has either lost or gained some *electrons*. Ions have a positive or negative electrical charge.

ionic bond A *bond* formed by the giving or receiving of *electrons* between *atoms*.

inorganic A term used to describe a *compound* that doesn't contain any carbon.

lattice A regular, interlocking network of *atoms*, *molecules* or *ions* inside a solid.

Law of Conservation of Mass A law stating that matter can't be created or destroyed, it can only change form.

mass number The total number of *protons* and *neutrons* in the *nucleus* of an *atom* of a certain *element*.

melting point The *temperature* at which a *substance* changes *state* from a solid to a liquid.

metal An *element* that conducts electricity and heat.

metalloid An *element* that shares *properties* with both *metals* and *non metals*.

mixture A collection of *elements* and/or *compounds* that have not bonded together.

molecule Two or more *atoms* bonded together. These *atoms* can be of one or more *elements*.

neutral A *substance* that is neither an *acid* nor a *base*, OR particles that have neither a positive nor a negative electrical charge.

neutralization reaction A *reaction* between an *acid* and a *base* that forms a *neutral* salt.

neutron A small, *neutral* particle found in the *nucleus* of an *atom*.

non metal An *element* that has no metal-like *properties*.

nucleus The centre of an *atom*, made up of *protons* and *neutrons*. The plural of nucleus is nuclei.

organic A term used to describe a *compound* that contains carbon.

oxidation When a *reactant* loses *electrons*.

Periodic Table A list of all known *elements* in order of increasing *atomic number*.

periods The rows of the *Periodic Table*. Going across the periods from left to right, *atoms* have more *protons*, *neutrons* and *electrons*.

pH A measure of how strong an *acid* or *base* is. A strong *acid* has a pH of 1 and a strong *base* has a pH of 14. A *neutral substance* has a pH of 7.

pressure The strength of *atoms* or *molecules* squashing against something.

product A *substance* formed by a *chemical reaction*.

properties The ways in which a *substance* behaves (physical properties) or *reacts* (chemical properties).

proton A small, positively charged particle found in the *nucleus* of an *atom*.

radiation Particles, light or heat rays given off by a *substance*. Not all radiation is harmful.

radioactive A term used to describe an unstable *substance* that emits harmful *radiation* as it breaks down.

rate of reaction The speed at which *reactants* turn into *products*.

reactant A *substance* that takes part in a *chemical reaction*.

reaction See *chemical reaction*.

redox reaction A *reaction* involving the *oxidation* of one *reactant* and the *reduction* of *another*.

reduction When a *reactant* gains *electrons*.

reversible reaction A *reaction* that can be reversed so the *products* change back into the *reactants*, usually by altering the *temperature* or *pressure*.

shell The path an *electron* takes as it moves around the *nucleus* of an *atom*'

solute A substance which is dissolved in a *solvent*.

solution A *mixture* of *substances* in a liquid.

solvent A liquid which *dissolves* another *substance* OR the liquid part of a *solution*.

state The form a *substance* takes – solid, liquid or gas.

steam Hot, gaseous water.

substances The different types of stuff the Universe is made of. Any solid, liquid or gas is a substance.

temperature A measure of how hot something is, usually given in °C (degrees Celsius).

water vapour Gaseous water, at any temperature.

Index

Acknowledgements

Every effort has been made trace and acknowledge ownership of copyright. If any rights have been omitted, the publishers offer to rectify this in any future editions following notification. The publishers are grateful to the following individuals and organizations for their permission to reproduce material on the following pages:

p16 Charles D. Winters/Science Photo Library (SPL); **p23** Charles D. Winters/SPL; **p65** © Robert Malone/Alamy; **p72** © Thom Lang/Corbis; **p73** bottom left SPL; bottom right Stefan Diller/SPL; **p80** Millard H. Sharp/SPL; **p82** © Weatherstock/Corbis; **p83** © Stephen Frink/Corbis; **p84** © Nick Greaves/Alamy

Series designer: Stephen Moncrieff
Art director: Mary Cartwright
With thanks to Brenda Cole and John Gillespie, MSc